Katherine Macalister

LAURA SECORD

THE
LEGEND
AND THE
LADY

With Best Wishes

Richard F. Record

LAURA SECORD

THE LEGEND AND THE LADY

RUTH McKENZIE

With a Portfolio of Illustrations

McCLELLAND AND STEWART LIMITED
Toronto/Montreal

0-7710-5819-5

THE CANADIAN PUBLISHERS

McClelland and Stewart Limited
25 Hollinger Road, Toronto 374

Printed and bound in Canada
by Maracle Press

CONTENTS

TO ESTHER SUMMERS

in appreciation of her generous assistance and lively interest in my search for the truth about our heroine.

ACKNOWLEDGMENTS

Many individuals contributed towards this book by providing source material, helping in research, conferring with the author, and reading the manuscript. My sincere thanks go to each and every one of them. Their co-operation was invaluable.

I am grateful also to the various archival institutions which gave me access to original documents pertaining to the life and times of Laura Secord: the Public Archives of Canada, the Ontario Department of Public Records and Archives, Queen's University Archives, the Niagara Historical Museum, and the Land Registry Offices at St. Catharines and Welland.

For permission to quote from historical publications I am indebted to the following: Buffalo and Erie County Historical Society, Lundy's Lane Historical Society, Niagara Historical Society, Ontario Historical Society, *Encyclopaedia Canadiana* representing the *Encyclopaedia of Canada* (edited by the late W. S. Wallace), McClelland and Stewart Limited, publisher of *The Gunners of Canada*, Volume I, by Colonel G. W. L. Nicholson, and University of Toronto Press, publisher of the *Canadian Historical Review*. The authors of the quotations are named in the appropriate places in the text, and those authors who are still living kindly gave their personal consent for the extracts to be quoted. I wish to thank authors and publishers alike for the privilege of quoting from their works. Finally, I should like in particular to express my appreciation of the splendid encouragement and support given to me by Mr. John Burke-Gaffney of London, Ontario, in the preparation and launching of this book.

Ottawa, May 6, 1971
R. McKenzie

People, Places, and Events in the Life of Laura Secord

A PORTFOLIO OF ILLUSTRATIONS
CONTEMPORARY TO THE PERIOD

Monument on the grave of Laura Secord in Drummond Hill Cemetery, Lundy's Lane, Niagara Falls. It was erected by the Ontario Historical Society in 1901. *Reproduced by courtesy of the Metropolitan Toronto Library Board.*

"The Battle of Queenston, 13th October, 1812." Drawn by Major J. B. Dennis and engraved by T. Sutherland. *Reproduced by courtesy of the Metropolitan Toronto Library Board.*

Robert Hamilton, 1750-1809, the founder of Queenston. *Portrait reproduced by courtesy of the Metropolitan Toronto Library Board.*

Laura Secord's home in Queenston, which is still situated on the north-west corner of Queen and Partition streets. From the watercolour by J. W. Cotton. (This house is being restored as a museum.) *Reproduced by courtesy of the Metropolitan Toronto Library Board.*

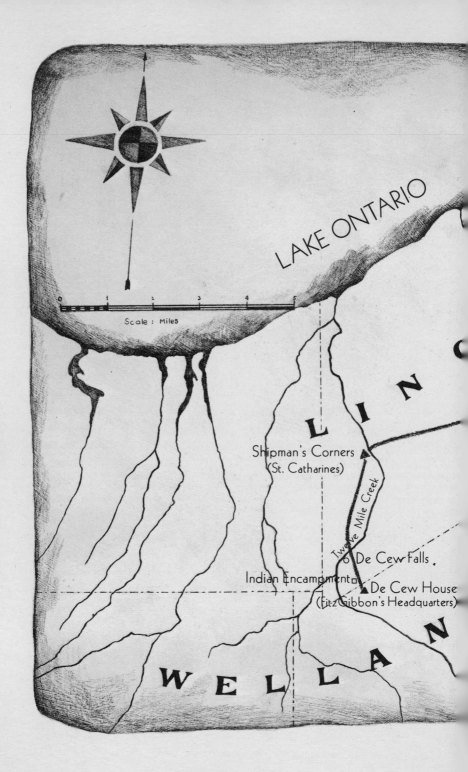

LAKE ONTARIO

Scale : Miles

LINC

Shipman's Corners
(St. Catharines)

Twelve Mile Creek

De Cew Falls

Indian Encampment

De Cew House
(FitzGibbon's Headquarters)

WELLAN

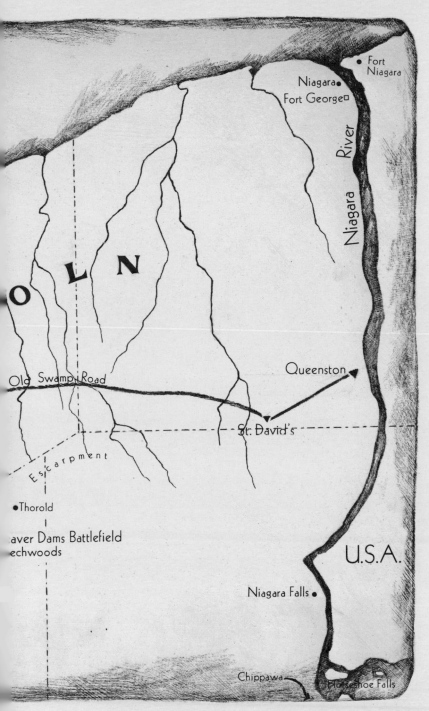

The above map traces the route Laura Secord is believed to have taken on her famous walk. *Illustration by Laszlo Gal.*

James Fitzgibbon, 1780-1863. *Portrait reproduced by courtesy of the Metropolitan Toronto Library Board.*

OPPOSITE UPPER: John De Cew's house, near Beaver Dams, where Fitzgibbon and his men had their headquarters. From the water-colour by J. W. Cotton. *Reproduced by courtesy of the Metropolitan Toronto Library Board.*

OPPOSITE LOWER: "Mrs. Secord Warning Fitzgibbon." A fanciful illustration from a woodcut by A. Bobbett. *Reproduced by courtesy of the Public Archives.*

Laura Secord's cottage at Chippawa, where she lived for twenty-seven years. From the watercolour by J. W. Cotton. *Reproduced by courtesy of the Metropolitan Toronto Library Board.*

OPPOSITE: Beaver Dams, 24th June 1813. Monument marking the burial place of the soldiers who died in the Battle of Beaver Dams, erected in 1874.

His Royal Highness Albert Edward, Prince of Wales, at the age of nineteen, the year he visited Canada. From a photograph by John Watkins, *Illustrated London News*, July 28, 1860.

Blondin's famous crossing of the Niagara river, carrying a man on his back. This extraordinary feat was part of the entertainment arranged during the Prince's visit to Canada. *Reproduced by courtesy of the Metropolitan Toronto Library Board.*

The first Sir Isaac Brock Monument. From a watercolour. *Reproduced by courtesy of the Metropolitan Toronto Library Board.*

Laura Ingersoll Secord as an old lady. From a woodcut. *Reproduced by courtesy of the Public Archives of Canada.*

The Laura Secord Monument at Queenston Heights, erected in 1910 by the Government of Canada. *Illustration by Laszlo Gal.*

PROLOGUE:
THE MYSTERY OF
LAURA SECORD

Fifty years ago there was no mystery about Laura
Secord; that is to say, puzzling questions were not
asked about her. She was accepted as the heroine of
the War of 1812. Everyone believed she had risked
her life to walk twenty miles through the woods to
warn Lieutenant James FitzGibbon of a surprise
attack by the Americans and that he had won the
Battle of Beaver Dams as a result.

Nineteenth-century biographers and poets exalted
Laura Secord as the great Canadian heroine, recount-
ing her deed in romantic and sentimental terms.
Monuments were erected to her memory.

Then came the questions. Skeptical historians
wanted to know how Mrs. Secord could have
obtained secret information about American plans.
What did her walk achieve? The message and the
walk were useless, they concluded, and went on to
"prove" that they were right.

Not everyone accepted this "proof" but it raised
doubts in many people's minds. The puzzle was two-
fold: If Laura Secord did take a warning to FitzGibbon (and even her detractors believed she did), how
had she acquired the information? And what part did
her message play in the victory at Beaver Dams?

As a person, Laura Secord has remained a

shadowy figure. In her best-known picture, the one that adorned a candy-box for many years, she appears old and grandmotherly, yet she was only thirty-seven at the time of her famous walk. To her admirers, Laura stands as the epitome of the pioneer Canadian woman — courageous, dauntless, resourceful. To other more cynical people she is something of a joke. The story that she drove a cow before her to fool the American sentries on her walk to Beaver Dams, strikes them as amusing. To such people, Laura tends to be more of a national joke than a national heroine.

What is the truth about Laura Secord? In the following pages the pieces of the puzzle are fitted together from documentary evidence, and the mystery surrounding her walk, her message, and her role in Canadian history is finally solved.

So let us turn back the clock to those far-off days over a century and a half ago when Canada was at war with the United States, and a young Queenston housewife undertook to warn a British officer of an impending enemy attack.

1/THE
WAR COMES
TO QUEENSTON

The thirteenth of October, 1812, was a day the people of Queenston would never forget. On that day the war came to their village.

Long before dawn on that chill, dull morning, hundreds of American soldiers slipped quietly into boats at Lewiston across the Niagara River and headed for Queenston. Though it is six miles north of Niagara Falls, the current is treacherous here and some of the American boats were caught in the eddy and carried downstream. Most of them made the crossing successfully and American soldiers were actually landing in the darkness before the sentry at Queenston observed them.

As soon as the alarm sounded, Captain James Dennis led his small force of fifty men down to the waterfront and opened fire. The 18-pounder gun at the redan battery half-way up the heights above the village started booming. The 24-pounder at Vrooman's Point, two miles to the north, joined in. Some of the shots found their targets and many American soldiers toppled from the boats into the water. About 200 landed at the Queenston wharf and sought shelter under the steep cliffs lining the shore. The waterfront became a nightmare of booming guns, flashing gunfire, wounded men tumbling into the river, and soldiers scrambling onto the wharf. Before daybreak, over 300 Americans had joined their leader under the cliffs. He was twenty-eight-year-old Captain John Wool. Over six feet tall and courageous, although inexperienced, the young officer had stepped into the breach when the American commander, Colonel Stephen Van Rensselaer had been forced to withdraw after being wounded four or five times soon after landing.

The noise of gunfire alarmed the villagers. Some 300 of them lived in houses on the main street above the docks and on a few streets farther back. The village seemed to nestle under the protection of the "mountain" which rises to the south and extends inland some distance towards the west. This high ridge is actually part of the Niagara escarpment.

In her bedroom under the gables of a neat, clapboard house on a street near the mountain, Mrs. James Secord wakened with a start. She sat up in bed, listening. There it was again — the sound of gunfire. Sometimes the explosion shook the house, then would come the answering cannon farther away, across the river. The dreaded attack had come! Laura thought of her husband, a sergeant in the first Lincoln militia regiment, now with Isaac Swayze's unit of artillery drivers. He would be in the thick of things.

The sound of marching feet, the clatter of horses' hooves, the gunfire and excited shouts coming from the docks, stirred the slender brown-haired Laura to action. She ran across the hall to the bedroom where the girls were sleeping and shook Mary and Charlotte (thirteen and ten) awake. They then roused and dressed six-year-old Harriet and three-year-old Charles while Laura looked after Appy (for Appolonia), the baby girl of two. In a few minutes all were ready and Laura led her family out the back

10

door into the lane behind the house. They shivered in the damp chilly air of early morning as they turned away from the village.

Laura and her little flock found their way through the mist along the familiar country road to a neighbouring farm, which lay about a mile away from the village, while "cannon balls were flying around in every direction," as she recalled in after years. There, at the farmhouse, Mrs. Secord and her children waited in suspense for most of that dreadful day.

They could tell from the booming of the guns that a battle was raging, but there was no telephone, no radio or television, to bring them news. Women, children and old men sat helplessly in farmhouses throughout the countryside, wondering what was happening to their loved ones. Sometimes there were tense periods of silence, only to be broken by the thunder of cannon, the rattle of musket-shots. Laura's face was pale and drawn as she worried about James. What would be the outcome?

At last, in the middle of the afternoon, the silence became prolonged, broken only occasionally by the sound of guns on the river banks. Laura could stand it no longer. Leaving the children at the farm, she hurried back to the village.

Three encounters with the enemy had taken place since Mrs. Secord and her children had fled from home that morning. The first two had ended disastrously for the British and Canadians. The third had brought them victory.

When the warning of the invasion had come to Major-General Isaac Brock at Fort George, six miles north of Queenston, he had hastily mounted his magnificent gray horse, Alfred, and set off at a gallop along the river road. The stalwart, forty-three-year-old British officer was in charge of the

11

defence of Upper Canada (Ontario). Already, at Detroit, he had demonstrated his boldness when, by a courageous but rash manoeuvre, he took the fort by surprise and persuaded General William Hull to surrender the fort and 2,300 men without even fighting. This victory had encouraged the Canadians to believe that perhaps, in spite of being overwhelmingly outnumbered, they might be able to resist their adversary. They loved and trusted General Brock.

On this October morning, as Brock spurred his horse along the road to Queenston, he paused briefly at Brown's Point, ordered the detachment of York militia which was guarding the gun-emplacement there to follow him into Queenston, and hastened on his way. At the village he quickly took stock of the situation. He summoned the unit of the 49th Regiment to descend from the redan battery on the heights to supplement the troops in the village, and then he rode up to the battery to see for himself what was happening on the river and the American shore. From the v-shaped parapet he observed American soldiers assembled across the river waiting for the boats to bring them over.

Suddenly bullets whizzed by and the general saw with dismay that American troops were actually at the top of the heights looking down on the battery. Captain Wool had led them up the cliff by an old fisherman's path which the British had thought unusable. Hastily ordering the 18-pounder gun to be spiked, Brock hurried down to the village with his gunners. By nine o'clock the men were ready to attack. Brock led them up the hill — men of the 49th Regiment and the Lincoln county militia — guiding them to the right of the redan battery so that Wool and his soldiers would be on their left, next to the river.

The advancing force had not gone far when a

bullet hit Brock in the wrist, but he paid little attention. He continued up the hill, leading his men. The tall officer presented a colourful picture in his red coat with the gold epaulettes and cocked hat, a perfect target in fact, and soon a soldier stepped from behind a tree, aimed his gun at Brock, and shot him in the chest. Brock fell and died almost at once. The men started back down the hill. Brock's aide-de-camp, Lieutenant-Colonel John Macdonell rallied the forces, and with some York militia who had just arrived, charged up the hill in a second attack, hoping to avenge Brock's death. Alas, his horse was shot from under him and he himself fell wounded. Dispirited, the British and Canadians retreated down the hill carrying Brock's body and the wounded Macdonell with them. According to tradition they left Brock's body, for the time being, in a stone house across the road from the Secord home. They took Macdonell to Durham's farm, a mile below the village. He died the next day. (The two heroes were buried at Fort George a few days later.)

By ten that morning, the Americans were sure the victory was theirs. On the heights, Captain Wool ordered his men to begin erecting fortifications to establish their position. Hundreds more soldiers crossed the river to Queenston in small boats despite the fire from the gun at Vrooman's Point. The defeated British and Canadians withdrew to Durham's farm where they waited for reinforcements from Fort George and Chippawa. A detachment of Royal Artillery soon arrived and joined the gunners at Vrooman's in an incessant barrage on the river.

In the afternoon, the counter-attack got under way. First the Indians, led by Lieutenant John Norton (a colourful Scotsman, married to an Indian girl, appointed Chief by the Five Nations and named as their Commander by General Brock). They climbed the heights from the southwest, and surprised the Americans at their work building fortifications. Emitting savage war whoops, guaranteed to frighten the enemy soldiers, the Indians began to skirmish with them, and succeeded in keeping them engaged until Major-General Roger Hale Sheaffe arrived with the main force.

Sheaffe, taking a roundabout route through the farmland back of the village, gained the heights without being seen by the Americans. With his combined force of troops from the 41st and 49th Regiments, a small company of Negroes from Niagara, units of the Lincoln and York militias, some cavalry and artillery, totalling altogether about 800 men, plus Norton's hundred or so Indians on his flank, Sheaffe advanced. Forming a long line stretching across the top of the hill, the troops moved towards the river forcing the enemy to swing around with their backs to the precipice, an impossible position for retreat. As the Americans were driven back towards the river, some of them panicked and began scrambling down the hill to the village, or over the cliffs to the river bank, where they hoped to be picked up by the boats. Many of them lost their lives falling over the cliffs.

Soon their commander, Colonel Winfield Scott, raised the white flag of surrender. By three-thirty in the afternoon the Battle of Queenston Heights was over. More than 300 soldiers and officers became prisoners on the spot. (By the next day this number was to swell to 900, as American soldiers who had been abandoned by their boats were rounded up in the village.)

But the victory held little happiness for the Secords. When Laura reached the village she heard

14

the grim news that her husband was lying wounded on the battlefield. Her dark eyes burning with anxiety she determined to go and find him and, breathing a prayer for divine assistance, she started to climb the hill.

She was horror-stricken by the sight of the battle-field with its scattered dead and wounded. The moans of the badly-wounded and dying men filled her with anguish. A good number of the fallen soldiers were Americans, easily recognizable by their blue tunics, but there were many in British red as well, and it was among these that Laura searched for James. When at last she found him, he was very weak and in great pain, with blood flowing from a wounded shoulder and with a bullet lodged in his knee. A kindly officer helped Laura get her husband down the hill and into their own house. Fortunately they had not far to go.

There is a family tradition that three American soldiers were about to club James to death just as his wife arrived on the scene. Captain Wool is said to have intervened, ordered the soldiers arrested, and instructed other soldiers to take Sergeant Secord home. But this story does not ring true. James Secord was wounded in the afternoon battle when Captain Swayze's artillery unit was in action. Secord belonged to the Car Brigade, a militia battery of field guns drawn by farm horses. When Laura climbed the hill, the British were in command of it, and Captain Wool, who had been badly wounded, had returned to Lewiston to get his wounds dressed. Mrs. Secord said, in a letter published years later, that she got James home "with the assistance of a Gentleman" and made no reference to the clubbing incident. Since this story has been attributed to Laura's grandson, James B. Secord, we may speculate that the elderly Mrs. Secord added imaginative details to her wartime experiences when relating them to her grandchildren.

Be that as it may, James Secord was a very sick man when his wife finally got him safely back into their own home. Here a further shock awaited them. The place had been looted in Laura's absence and everything was in chaos. (The looting had occurred during a lull in the fighting around noon, at which time some American soldiers had broken into the deserted homes of the villagers and plundered them.) However, in spite of the disorder surrounding her Laura managed to get James into bed and to bathe and dress his wound.

The following days must have been a great strain, both physically and mentally, for Laura as she nursed her husband, and continued to pray to God for his recovery. It was probably a great relief when he was finally well enough to be moved and the family departed for St. David's, where they spent the winter.

James had been raised in this village, which was only three miles from Queenston, and he and Laura had lived there when they were first married. Indeed it might have been called "Secordville" because a number of Secords had settled on farms in the immediate area. It had actually been named after a Secord — James' older brother David — who owned a farm, mills and shops. Another brother, Stephen, had also been one of the original settlers and had owned a mill, but he had died four years before the war. However, his widow, Hannah, with her children (who ranged in age from seven to twenty-seven) still lived in St. David's and continued to run the mill.

Surrounded by so many in-laws and old friends, Laura did not lack for assistance in taking care of her husband, and James was able to convalesce comfortably and recover slowly from his wound.

16

2/LAURA'S GIRLHOOD AND MARRIAGE

As the Secord family waited out the winter of 1812-13 at St. David's, Laura's thoughts must have turned at times to other troubled periods in her life. She had, in fact, seldom been free of trouble, for she first saw the light of day the year the American Revolution erupted in the battles of Lexington, Concord and Bunker Hill, and in the very state where these battles took place.

Laura Ingersoll was born in Great Barrington, Massachusetts, on September 13, 1775, the first child of twenty-six-year-old Thomas Ingersoll and his wife, Elizabeth Dewey, a girl of seventeen. The couple had been married in February of the same year, and those who count months in such cases will see that the required number was short by two. This is probably why some biographers have said that Laura was born in December, 1775. In her own time, her birthday was celebrated on September 13, and this was the date placed on the original marble slab that marked her grave in Drummond Hill Cemetery.

The years of the American Revolution were tumultuous ones in which to live. Young men like Thomas Ingersoll had to choose which side to fight for — the British Loyalist or the "colonial patriot."

17

It was no easy choice. Joining the Loyalists meant being branded as a traitor and subjected to violent persecution. Many Loyalists had their buildings burned, their cattle driven off or their property seized, while they themselves were captured and imprisoned, perhaps even tarred and feathered or forced to ride a rail through town, before being locked up. If possible, they escaped and went to New York to join the Loyalist army or fled to Canada where their families found shelter while the men fought in one of the Loyalist regiments.

Feelings against the British ran particularly high in Massachusetts. It was in the capital city of that colony where the Boston tea party had taken place. So it is not surprising that the young Thomas Ingersoll chose the "home team" — the patriots or revolutionaries. From 1777 until the end of the war he was an officer in the state force of Massachusetts, rising to the rank of captain. When Shay's Rebellion broke out in the state a few years after the war, Captain Ingersoll helped to put it down and was promoted to major.

Laura Ingersoll never knew what it meant to have a carefree childhood, overshadowed as it was by war. One can imagine the tearful farewells that must have taken place every time her father left home in his captain's uniform — how his young wife clung to him, weeping, as she bade him adieu, fearing that she might never again see him alive, or that he might return wounded or crippled. The child Laura must have dreaded these farewells as she too kissed her father good-bye. Her mother must have seemed doubly precious as the one she could always count on to be there, in the home. What a shock it must have been, then, when Elizabeth Ingersoll died, leaving Laura to take care of her three little sisters. She was then only eight years old.

A year later Thomas Ingersoll married again. His second wife was spared to him only four years, and died childless. Within a few months Thomas took as his third wife, Sarah Whiting, who became the mother of his second family of four sons and three daughters. Before Laura was fifteen she had had three different mothers — a disturbing experience for any young girl.

Laura grew up fair of skin, with abundant light brown hair, expressive dark eyes and a slender figure. Of medium height, with a small frame and fair complexion, she looked delicate and fragile. Time would show how deceptive this appearance was. Laura Ingersoll was made of tough and durable fibre that was to stand the test of many trials to come. Neither her strength nor her courage ever failed her.

Times were hard in Massachusetts in the years following the revolution. When Laura was eighteen, her father decided to turn his back on the young republic and move to Upper Canada. He had heard about the generous terms on which land was available in the new province. Perhaps also he was disillusioned with the republican government.

With four associates, Thomas Ingersoll drew up a petition asking Lieutenant-Governor John Graves Simcoe for a township grant in Upper Canada. Thomas made the long and tedious journey in March, 1793, to the seat of government at Newark (Simcoe's name for Niagara) to present the petition in person. In return for the land grant, the group of associates agreed to bring in a minimum of forty families as settlers within seven years. Each family would receive two hundred acres of land for a nominal land fee.

Governor Simcoe and Council approved the grant, saying that the petitioner, Thomas Ingersoll, "comes precisely under that description of persons who ought to be encouraged to settle in this Province." The township Ingersoll chose was on the Thames River and was called Oxford-upon-the Thames (now North, East and West Oxford townships).

It took Ingersoll two years to wind up his affairs in Massachusetts and move his family to Canada. The journey was a difficult and hazardous one to make with a family of small children. Great Barrington was about twenty-five miles from the Hudson River — a day's drive by wagon or stage-coach. After a night's rest at an inn or with relatives, the family no doubt boarded a sloop for the sail up the Hudson River to Albany, where they transferred to a coach for the ten-mile overland journey to Schenectady. There the weary travellers descended from the jolting horse-drawn vehicle and hired a flat-bottomed Durham boat which they had to propel by poles and oars against the strong current of the Mohawk River. This brought them, after a portage, to the Oswego River and thence to the port of Oswego on the southeastern shore of Lake Ontario. By this time, their bones were aching from the cramped and crowded quarters of the Durham boat, and they were glad to move to a schooner which would take them to the western end of Lake Ontario.

But further troubles lay ahead. The sailing vessel tossed and rolled on the ocean-like waves of the lake, and as it neared its destination the sails were becalmed. A violent storm arose and the passengers, fearing to be capsized, went ashore and put up a tent for shelter. Provisions were scarce by this time and they realized that the delay could mean severe suffering and near-starvation, especially for the children. The men struck out through the woods to try to find food, and a distant light beckoned them to a hunter's camp. The hunters had no food to give them but they led the way to a settler's house where milk and other provisions were obtained. After the storm, the boat proceeded on its way.

Where did the boat finally land? No one knows for sure. Some people say the Ingersolls went to Burlington at the head of Lake Ontario, then by Indian trail to Oxford township. But the township was a wilderness at the time, without roads and only partially surveyed, so the mother and children could not have gone by that route. More likely the boat landed at Niagara where Thomas had been before, or it may have gone on to Queenston. Certainly, that is where Thomas Ingersoll was established in November, 1795, operating a tavern.

Like many men of his day, Major Ingersoll was a Jack-of-all-trades, not well educated but highly resourceful. He went to Oxford township as soon as he could, to claim his land. He then built a log house "on the 20th Lot on the River Thames," which eventually became the site of the town of Ingersoll. Thomas returned to Queenston to wait until the survey and roads would make settlement possible. He had to build the first road for settlers himself and he hired Charles Whiting, his brother-in-law, to mark out the concessions. Mr. Whiting used Ingersoll's log house as the base from which he did his surveying in October, 1796. Two streams flowing into the Thames River were named "Ingersoll Creek" and "Whiting Creek" in memory of the two pioneers. Settlers began to move into the township the year the survey took place.

Meanwhile Ingersoll kept his tavern in Queenston as a source of much-needed cash. The tiny village was an ideal location for an inn. It was the northern terminus of the Portage Road, over which freight was hauled to bypass the falls and rapids in the

Niagara River. Boats arriving from Montreal, Kingston and York (Toronto), unloaded their cargoes at "the Landing" (Queenston's original name) and piled them on to wagons to be taken across country to Chippawa, three miles beyond the Falls. What a sight it must have been to see the "trains" of wagons loaded with barrels, bags and wooden boxes, drawn by four or five yoke of slow-moving oxen, or by teams of horses in double or triple span. On some days as many as sixty wagons were loaded at Queenston for transport along this road.

Queenston was thus a bustling little centre for trading and forwarding. Some of the food and merchandise arriving there by boat was traded by the merchants among the farmers and villagers. Similarly Chippawa, at the other end of the Portage Road, was a distributing centre for the people of that area. Most of the freight that arrived there, however, was loaded once again onto boats for delivery to places on Lake Erie and the upper lakes. The reverse traffic brought furs and farm produce to Queenston for trade in city markets along Lake Ontario and the St. Lawrence River.

Queenston had been founded in 1791 to meet the need for port facilities on the west side of the Niagara River after the British had relinquished the east side to the Americans in the peace treaty that brought the American War of Independence to an end. Wharves and warehouses were built at this "new Landing" and work was begun on the Portage Road.

The founder of the village and chief builder of the Portage Road was Robert Hamilton, a Scottish immigrant who became the biggest landowner, the most prominent merchant, and the leading public official of the Niagara district. In addition to his mercantile activities, Hamilton had a farm, a distillery and a tannery at Queenston and business interests at Chippawa. His outstanding ability was recognized by Lieutenant-Governor Simcoe who appointed him to the first Legislative Council of Upper Canada, made him a judge of the Court of Common Pleas and a member of the district Land Board. Hamilton was, indeed, the father figure of the district or, as they said in those days, "the squire." His two-storey stone house, high on the river bank, overlooked the village from its porticoed front, while the back rooms commanded a magnificent view of the river and the American shore. Set in the midst of fruit and shade trees, the house impressed travellers with its substantial elegance. All the dignitaries who went to see Niagara Falls, called on the Hamiltons. The Duke of Kent (Queen Victoria's father) had lunch at the Hamilton home on his journey to Niagara as a young man. Governor Simcoe and his wife were frequent visitors, though the swarthy Scot with his prominent nose, striking dark eyes and determined chin was too independent in his thinking to please the Governor entirely, and there was friction between them. Their wives were devoted to each other. Mrs. Hamilton (she was Robert's first wife) was Catherine Askin Robertson, daughter of the well-known merchant and fur trader, John Askin and *his* first wife, an Indian girl.

It was probably Governor Simcoe who gave the Landing its name of "Queenstown," but whether this was done in honour of his regiment, the Queen's Rangers, or for Queen Charlotte, wife of King George the Third, is not known. The Queen's Rangers were stationed in the village for a time. In a letter written in August, 1792, the Lieutenant-Governor said, "I have found it most adviseable to hut the Queen's Rangers at the New Landing upon the Niagara River." Three months later, on

November 4, 1792, he reported that the "Queen's Rangers are hutted by great exertions at the Niagara Landing, now Queenstown." By March, 1793, the name had been shortened in official records to "Queenston." Travellers referred to the village by different versions of its two names.

A famous traveller, the Duc de la Rochefoucault-Liancourt, who passed through "Queen's Town" in June, 1795, described it as having "a tolerable inn, two or three good storehouses, a blockhouse of stone, covered with iron, and barracks, which should be occupied by the regiment of General Simcoe, but which are now unoccupied." The "tolerable inn" was no doubt Fairbank's Tavern. The Ingersolls had not yet arrived.

A village tavern at that time was a community centre. Not only did men enjoy conviviality over their drinks, they often held meetings there. An early Masonic lodge, No. 19, held its first meeting in Fairbank's Tavern in May, 1795. Later, the lodge met from time to time in Ingersoll's Tavern beginning in November, 1795 and on through 1796 and 1797. Thomas Ingersoll joined the lodge himself in 1796.

This is of particular interest to our story, because the young James Secord had become a Freemason in the same lodge a year earlier. Was it through the Masonic bond that the Secords and Ingersolls became friends? No doubt James and Ingersoll also had business relations.

How James and Laura first became acquainted remains a mystery, but in a small place like Queenston newcomers to the village were readily welcomed by the older settlers. The Ingersolls would not be long in Queenston before they would be invited to people's homes, to parties and community gatherings. One writer, who compiled a list of

24

"belles of the day" in Niagara, from 1792 to 1800, included a Miss Ingersoll and three Miss Secords, without mentioning their first names. Presumably the Miss Ingersoll was Laura and the Miss Secords would be sisters or cousins of James.

The date of James' and Laura's wedding is also unknown, but it seems likely the event took place in 1797 before Thomas took his family to the log house in Oxford-upon-the-Thames. One might have expected that the marriage ceremony would have been performed by the Reverend Robert Addison, Church of England clergyman at Niagara. Ministers of other denominations were not permitted to perform marriages in those days, and Addison was the nearest clergyman to Queenston. However the record of marriages performed by Mr. Addison in the 1790s and early 1800s does not include the names of Laura Ingersoll and James Secord.

It therefore follows that the young couple were probably married by a justice of the peace, perhaps by James' brother David. It was quite common for magistrates to perform marriages and the reason they were permitted to do so was because of the shortage of clergymen of the official faith. "When a wedding took place they formed a little party and would travel to the nearest Justice of the Peace, who quietly performed the ceremony according to Law," wrote Colonel John Clark, a militia veteran of the War of 1812. Major David Secord himself, was twice married by a justice of the peace, and he held this office in his community. As such he must have officiated at many weddings. His records were undoubtedly burned in the fire of 1814, set by enemy troops, which wiped out the village of St. David's and Major Secord's house, farm buildings and mills. This would account for the lack of marriage record in the case of James and Laura Secord.

James Secord had a 200-acre farm which he had received as a United Empire Loyalist grant. His father, Lieutenant James Secord, had been one of the original settlers at Niagara, a member of Colonel John Butler's corps of Rangers who were the first Loyalists to come to Upper Canada. In 1777, Lieutenant Secord brought to Fort Niagara (on the American side but then in British hands) "forty six Loyal subjects all which joined his Majesty's standard." The following year, he brought his family "consisting of a Wife and seven Children, three of which joined Col'l Butler's Rangers." James junior was only five at the time.

The Secords were of French Huguenot descent. In France, the family was known as "Sicard," and the original immigrant, Ambroise Sicard, came to New York in 1686. His descendant, Lieutenant James Secord, settled on his land grant in Niagara township (on the Canadian side) at the close of the American Revolutionary War. He died, unfortunately, in 1784, leaving his widow, the former Madelaine (or Magdalen) Badeau, five sons and three daughters. (The eldest son, Solomon, was then twenty-nine. He was probably with the Rangers before his father came to Niagara). The four sons, Solomon, Stephen, David and James all settled in the Niagara area. Another son, John, was said to have disappeared, no one knew where. A daughter, Magdalen, married the distinguished Kingston businessman and public figure, Richard Cartwright, a friend and business associate of Robert Hamilton's. James Secord, born in 1773, was the youngest of the family.

James and Laura, as bride and groom, lived at St. David's. Sometime later they moved to Queenston. The young couple went through a period of severe financial strain in their early married life. James had gone into business as a merchant in 1795 and had difficulty making ends meet. His chief source of supply for goods was his brother-in-law, Richard Cartwright, who, with his greater experience and shrewd business sense, offered sound advice: do not give credit. "It is generally better to have the goods [on hand] than outstanding Debts," he wrote to James. "Much of a mans future Success in Life depends upon the Prudence & Caution with which he sets out." James was only twenty-two, fourteen years junior to Cartwright.

Whether or not James heeded the advice not to extend credit, we do not know, but he himself depended on credit in making his purchases and he ran badly into debt. In a letter to one of his creditors, written in November, 1798, James said, "I have not a Shilling in my possession at this Moment. I am just now setting out for York where I hope to get some money . . . & what is a little astonishing, I have not a shilling in my pockets to pay my passage over."

A year later James explained to another creditor, Robert Macaulay, a Kingston merchant, that he was unable to pay the note that had come due. In his letter he made his first known reference to his wife when he said in conclusion, "Mrs. Secord & my own best complements to you & Mrs. Macaulay. . . ." The Macaulays and Cartwrights were old friends. When Mr. Macaulay died suddenly in 1800, Richard Cartwright became an executor of his will.

James Secord owed money to another business connection of Cartwright's in Montreal, the prominent merchants James and Andrew McGill. (James McGill became the founder of McGill University.)

These debts worried Cartwright who was one of the smartest business men in early Upper Canada. Although money was scarce and there were few settlers in the province, this United Empire Loyalist built up the largest retail outlet in Kingston, and became one of the leading traders and forwarders on the St. Lawrence. His friend, Reverend (later Bishop) John Strachan, described him as a man of "strict probity and inviolable love of truth," a man who appeared "distant and reserved" to strangers but who never deserted any of his friends. Like Robert Hamilton, Cartwright was prominent in public life. He was a member of the first Legislative Council of Upper Canada, a judge of the Court of Common Pleas, and a justice of the peace. Lieutenant-Governor Simcoe commissioned him Lieutenant of Frontenac County, a form of office that disappeared with Simcoe's return to England in 1796.

Cartwright was critical of James Secord's business practices. Writing to the McGill brothers in 1799, he said: "Inclosed is a letter from my Kinsman Mr. Secord who has some thoughts of setting up a Potasherie which may probably answer well enough. — You will see by his letter that he does not want Candour; and I can answer for his Honesty & Industry; though I do not choose to become responsible for his Success further than I am already." On the same date he wrote James, rebuking him for going into debt. "If you are not a little more circumspect," he said, "it will be of little Consequence what Plans you follow; for none can ever succeed." Two years later he warned James, " . . . it is absolutely necessary that the Debt of Jas. and A. McGill should be soon extinguished." Cartwright felt so strongly about this that he took over part of Secord's debt to the McGills. This, on top of what James owed him in business transactions, added up to 800 pounds (about $2,000), a large sum of money in those days. In 1801, James mortgaged his farm to Cartwright in payment of this debt. His wife Laura appeared before a judge at Niagara to sign away her "claim of Dower in & out of the within granted Lands."

By 1812, according to James Secord's own recollections some twenty years later, he had become a merchant in Queenston "in easy circumstances." The correspondence with his brother-in-law indicates that he dealt as a wholesaler in flour, potash and other products. Perhaps he also did forwarding. It seems doubtful, however, if he ever got out of debt. He and Laura, with their five children, lived, as we have seen, in a clapboard house under the shadow of Queenston Heights. This comfortable but modest storey-and-a-half house still stands on the corner of Queen and Partition Streets, but has been considerably altered over the years.* The "storehouse" used for merchandise was a block away at the intersection of Partition, Front and Prince (now Princess) Streets.

Meanwhile Laura's father had failed to fulfil his commitment in Oxford-upon-the-Thames. He had received twelve hundred acres of land for himself, had opened up the township but had not brought in the required number of settlers. His four associates had not even put in an appearance. Worse still, government land policy had changed after Governor Simcoe left Upper Canada. Townships were no longer granted as a whole and the government cancelled Ingersoll's contract on the ground that he had not kept his bargain. The upshot was that Thomas Ingersoll became discouraged and disillusioned. He pulled up stakes in Oxford and moved to the Credit River in 1805. There, on the site of Port Credit, he operated an inn known as "Government House."

*The Laura Secord Candy Shops bought this house in 1969 with a view to restoration.

This inn had been built by the government of Upper Canada to accommodate judges and other officials who had to go to the provincial capital of York (Toronto) to attend the courts or on other government business. York was then a muddy village, raw and isolated in comparison with the older settlements of the Niagara district. Travellers found a welcome haven at the Government House, conveniently located ten miles west of York, at the mouth of the Credit River. Whether they came by boat via Lake Ontario, on horseback or by coach over the east-west Lakeshore Road, or whether they were fur traders coming on foot down the old Indian trail from the back country, they were glad to see the sturdy inn with the welcoming puffs of smoke emerging from its chimneys.

The Government House was built of squared logs clapboarded over. On each side of the building were four large windows, with many small panes, and on the peaked roof were two large chimney stacks made of stones from the Credit River bed. The ground floor contained two large front rooms and some smaller rooms at the back. A few bedrooms were located under the eaves in the attic.

Thomas Ingersoll leased the Government House for seven years. It made a comfortable home and a good living for his large family. By this time he had six daughters and four sons. The youngest son, James, was four when the family moved to the Credit. Sarah, the youngest daughter, was born in 1807. Laura, the eldest of the family, and her three sisters, Elizabeth, Mira and Abigail, were married before this baby was born. Before the seven-year lease expired, Thomas Ingersoll had died. It was 1812. The widow, "Sally" Ingersoll, and her son Charles, applied for a renewal of the lease. Charles was already actively engaged in the war and his mother carried on the inn herself. A few years later, the Ingersolls left the Credit. Charles returned to Oxford-upon-the-Thames in 1817, repurchased his father's farm at a sheriff's sale, and, with his younger brother Thomas, built a new house, mills, a store and a potashery. They named the new village "Ingersoll" in memory of their father. Charles became the first postmaster of Ingersoll in 1821, and was succeeded by his youngest brother James in 1834.

But this is getting ahead of our story. Long before the propitious founding of Ingersoll, the War of 1812 had erupted, and Charles Ingersoll and the Secords were deeply involved in it. As we have seen, the Battle of Queenston Heights left James Secord badly wounded, a circumstance that would impel his wife to perform the deed that made her famous.

3/LIFE
GOES ON IN
THE MIDST
OF WAR

The winter of 1812-13 was a quiet one on the Niagara frontier. Most of the war action took place in the east, on Lake Ontario and the St. Lawrence. As a matter of fact, only three battles of the entire War of 1812 had a direct bearing on the Laura Secord episode; these were the battles of Queenston Heights, Stoney Creek and Beaver Dams. But in a general way the war affected everyone.

What was it like to live in those days? War, certainly, was very different from the mechanized, impersonal kind we know today — General Brock was killed by a bullet aimed directly at him. There were no machine-guns, no tanks, no air raids, no threat of atomic bombs. Soldiers moved on foot or on horseback, bearing old-fashioned muskets and bayonets. Heavy field-guns were mounted on wheels and, when it was necessary to move them, they were attached to limbers pulled by four- or six-horse teams. The limbers resembled carts and carried the ammunition.

Between battles people resumed their everyday activities. Nevertheless everyone's life was disorganized. Family life was broken up, farming was carried on with the greatest difficulty, and trade was disrupted. We have already seen that at Queenston people's homes were plundered. This sort of thing happened to many people, sometimes more than once, as it did, in fact, with the Secords ". . . the Enemy having possession of the Frontier, from time to time gained possession of his [Secord's] residence and plundered him of every article they thought fit to carry away," James Secord was to state years later in a petition to the government. Niagara was burned in December 1813, and St. David's in July 1814. The countryside was ravaged by marching troops. Where they encamped they dug field entrenchments and refuse pits. They burned rail fences for fuel, destroyed bridges, and ruined the rough pioneer roads with the transport of their heavy guns and ammunition.

Every family saw its able-bodied men go off to fight in the militia. These units were attached mainly to the infantry but there were also special corps like the artillery drivers and the cavalry. Lincoln county had five militia regiments and a unit of artillery drivers. As the county, and indeed the entire province, were predominantly agricultural, most of the volunteers came from farms and they were constantly worried about their crops and livestock. While they were away the women stayed home to manage on their own. They had to cope not only with farm operations but with marauding troops, visits from Indians who demanded food and accommodation for the night, and other unexpected hazards such as fires. Whenever there was a lull between battles the militiamen were allowed to go home to their farms. Even without permission, many went home so concerned were they about the seeding and harvest. Food production was essential to the cause, so who could blame them?

When the war started, there were fears that recent American immigrants of non-Loyalist origin, might prove traitors to Canada, and in truth some did. A number returned to the United States; and some who stayed in Canada for a time, co-operated with the invader or defected to the American forces. The great majority remained loyal to Canada and joined in defending their homes and adopted country.

The Ingersolls had an American revolutionary background. Where did they stand? Thomas Ingersoll died in 1812 as has been said, and his wife and younger children remained at the inn on the Credit River. There could be no question of the eldest daughter's loyalty. Married to a United Empire Loyalist who had also been an officer in the militia (James Secord had been a captain in the First Lincoln Militia regiment, had resigned, and then re-enlisted in 1812 with the rank of sergeant), and the mother of five children born in Upper Canada, Laura Ingersoll Secord had become "Canadian." The course of events would show how strong her loyalty was.

Charles Ingersoll, Laura's half-brother, was the oldest son of the family. He was twenty-one when war broke out. The next son, Thomas, was only sixteen. Charles volunteered as a cavalryman in Thomas Merritt's Niagara Light Dragoons and participated in the Battle of Queenston Heights. Charles has not recorded his impressions of this battle but perhaps he reacted much like his future brother-in-law, William Hamilton Merritt, son of Major Thomas Merritt, who tells in his *Memoirs* what the battle meant to him and his fellow cavalrymen.

Nineteen-year-old Hamilton Merritt was a lieutenant in the dragoons. He was stationed at Fort George (just south of Niagara, now Niagara-on-the-Lake), when word came that the enemy had landed at Queenston. Filled with excitement at the thought of their first clash with the enemy, the troop of cavalry galloped over the six-mile stretch of road to Queenston. While on their way they heard the shocking news that General Brock had been killed. They met their own county militiamen retreating from the battle and saw the wounded being carried to safety. "In short, for young soldiers," Merritt wrote, "we had the most dismal prospects before us that can possibly be conceived."

That afternoon their spirits rose when General Sheaffe overcame the Americans on the heights and took as prisoners the defeated soldiers and officers. Merritt said,

> It would be impossible to describe the feelings of our young soldiers at this moment, having entered the action with the idea, even if successful of at least two thirds being killed or wounded. In 10 minutes, to have all the enemy that were not killed, in our possession, with a loss on our part of not more than 12 or 13 men.* It was the most fortunate circumstance for us, giving new life to everything around us.

The enthusiastic Lieutenant Merritt became captain in command of the Niagara Provincial Light Dragoons when the corps was reorganized in the spring of 1813 and his father Thomas Merritt retired. Charles Ingersoll was promoted to lieutenant in this corps. He remained with the Niagara Dragoons until the war came to an end in the fall of 1814. (Two years later he married Merritt's sister, Anna Maria. W. H. Merritt became a prominent politician and the leading promoter of the Welland Canal).

---

*Actually 14 were killed, 77 wounded, exclusive of Indians, and 21 were missing.

There was a curiously friendly aspect to the War of 1812. After all, Americans and Canadians had been neighbours and friends until war was declared by the remote governments in Washington and London. The following story illustrates this side of the war.

In the summer of 1812, a Queenston farmer sold a cow to a man at Lewiston. The farmer sent the cow on the Queenston ferry to her new owner in the States. But the cow, so the story goes, was loyal to the British cause and preferred to live on the Canadian side. One day she wandered down to the river, looked solemnly at its turbulent waters, decided to chance it, plunged in and swam across to Queenston. There she remained with her former owner for the duration of the war.

"It was often a source of great merriment to both parties," wrote Colonel John Clark in recollecting this episode, "bulletins passing to and fro occasionally that her ladyship was in excellent health, and enjoying herself, notwithstanding the roar of cannon and musket balls that kept flying at times over her head."

This story may be far-fetched but it is symbolic of the feeling of friendship that persisted among many people on the two sides of the river, despite the battles fought in the war.

There were frequent contacts too between Canadian settlers and American soldiers who were encamped in the neighbourhood. Sometimes the Americans would drop into a house or an inn and demand food and drink. The Canadian hosts were not above playing tricks on their guests. A villager of St. David's recalled that once when American troops were passing through, he had pocketed over a hundred dollars from the sale of whiskey. "I had a barrel of whiskey and a barrel of water," he said.

"As the whiskey was sold I kept replenishing with water, and towards the last it would not have hurt your conscience to sell a drink of it, for it was so weak it could hurt no one."*

This was the lighter side of the war, but mostly it was deadly serious, and as the spring of 1813 opened up, the war gained momentum. At first the British and Canadians got off to a bad start. In April, the Americans landed at what is now Sunnyside Beach, Toronto, seized Fort York, and burned the Parliament Buildings and Government House (where the Lieutenant-Governor lived).

Fort George was the next to fall. American naval boats at Fort Niagara, just across the river, set fire to the log buildings of the fort by cannonading across the river. On May 27, the fleet crossed the river and, under protection of its shelling, the American army, led by Colonel Winfield Scott, landed on the Canadian side. The British suffered severe casualties (over fifty killed and 300 wounded or missing) and the commander, Brigadier-General John Vincent, withdrew the troops from the fort rather than suffer complete destruction by being bottled up within. He ordered the guns to be spiked and the ammunition destroyed, and then marched his men to the supply depot in Captain John De Cew's stone house near Beaver Dams, about eighteen miles to the southwest. Next day Vincent sent the militia home and took his regular troops to Burlington Heights at the head of Lake Ontario.

A corps of American soldiers and cavalry pursued Vincent as far as Stoney Creek on the south shore of Lake Ontario. This gave the British an opportunity to retaliate. A small force under Lieutenant-Colonel John Harvey moved from Burlington

*Emma A. Currie, *The Story of Laura Secord, and Canadian Reminiscences* (Toronto, Briggs, 1900), p. 138.

Heights after midnight on June 6, and attacked the Americans where they were encamped in a field at Stoney Creek. They bayoneted the sentries and burst in on the sleeping soldiers. In the dark the fighting became confused. The battle ended before daylight with "both parties leaving the scene of action, each believing the others the conquerors," Lieutenant James FitzGibbon said. But it was as good as a victory for the British, because the Americans retired to Forty Mile Creek (now Grimsby). The next day, when a squadron of British ships on Lake Ontario threatened to cut off American communications, the Americans withdrew to Fort George.

General Vincent then moved all his troops from Burlington Heights to Forty Mile Creek. Some military men criticized him for not pursuing the Americans all the way to Fort George. One of these was James FitzGibbon. According to his granddaughter, Mary Agnes FitzGibbon, it was he who had reconnoitered the layout of the American encampment at Stoney Creek in preparation for the surprise attack. Disguising himself as a settler with a basket of butter to sell, he visited the American camp, cracked jokes with the soldiers, gave them "confidential information" on the British forces, all the while casting his sharp eyes around the camp. This may be a romantic description of FitzGibbon's performance but it is in keeping with his colourful personality.

Lieutenant James FitzGibbon was an energetic and aggressive man who had no patience with what seemed to him Vincent's passivity. "I expected every hour to see waggons brought to carry forward our Troops in pursuit, but we were not advanced for two days after [the Battle of Stoney Creek], when we were marched to the 40 Mile

Creek and there halted. This tardiness suggested to me the idea of offering myself to serve in advance of the Army with 50 Chosen men to be employed where and how I might please."

FitzGibbon obtained permission to do this, and he hand-picked his men from among the most daring and trustworthy of his own 49th Regiment. They were all men he knew well. On the night of June 12, he marched with his unit to his new headquarters at De Cew's house.

This was a large two-storey house, very grand and modern in its day. It had been built just before the war by John De Cew, a captain in the Lincoln militia. The house stood on the escarpment not far from present-day De Cew Falls and about two miles west of the settlement of Beaver Dams. It was built of native limestone, with stairway, doors and panelling of black walnut, and heated by huge fireplaces big enough to burn logs. Part of the walls and fireplaces may still be seen today.* Some of the gnarled old trees in the spacious grounds are still standing.

It was John De Cew's second house. As an early United Empire Loyalist settler, De Cew had first built a log cabin on his land. He was an enterprising settler, one of the first farmers to experiment with fruit trees and he was destined to become a leading citizen of the Niagara Peninsula. He met the needs of pioneers by building grist, saw and flaxseed-oil mills, utilizing the water-power from the falls that now bear his name. (The name, pronounced De Koo, is of French Huguenot origin and was spelled in a variety of ways: De Cew, De Cou, De Cow and even De Camp.)

At the outbreak of the war, John De Cew lent his house to the British as a supply depot for arms

---

*The house was burned in 1950. The property is owned by the Ontario Hydro-Electric Power Commission.

and ammunition. His mills were used to grind grain for the troops. After the Americans took Fort George, a raiding party captured Captain De Cew along with a number of other men of the area. The prisoners were "hurried across the river to Batavia," then forced to march on foot to Albany, New York, a distance of some three hundred miles, where they were put in internment camps. Eventually De Cew escaped but it was 1814 before he returned home. In the meantime, Mrs. De Cew and the children continued living in some upstairs rooms of the stone house while FitzGibbon and his men used it as a base for their activities.

By this time, the middle of June 1813, James and Laura Secord with their four girls and one little boy, had returned to their home in Queenston. James was still suffering from his wounds. His shoulder bothered him to the end of his days, and the bullet in his knee was never removed.

4/ THE SECRET PLAN TO CAPTURE FITZGIBBON

The Niagara Peninsula was now a kind of no-man's land. The Americans, in the key position at Fort George, controlled the entrance to the Niagara River and had outposts extending southward from the fort, dominating the road to Queenston. Further west, the British had stationed three detachments on the south side of Lake Ontario overlooking the Niagara countryside. The main British force under General John Vincent was still at Forty Mile Creek. Lieutenant-Colonel Cecil Bisshopp was in charge of another post at Twenty Mile Creek, while Major P. V. De Haren commanded the advanced post near Ten Mile Creek.* Lieutenant FitzGibbon's unit at De Cew's house served as a fourth outpost, the point of the British triangle. Neither the British nor the Americans had a firm grip on the whole peninsula.

When Lieutenant FitzGibbon established his fifty-man force at De Cew's house, he had two objects in mind: to observe the enemy's movements, and to harass him as much as possible. He had learned from

---

*These places (and the creeks on which they stood), were named according to their distance from the Niagara River, hence Forty Mile Creek, now Grimsby; Twenty Mile Creek, Jordan; Twelve Mile Creek, St. Catharines; Ten Mile Creek, Homer; and Four Mile Creek, Virgil.

the Indians how to utilize the woods for guerilla tactics, surprising the enemy while protecting oneself. This kind of warfare appealed to his sense of adventure.

James FitzGibbon was a highly spirited person. In a day when officers' commissions were purchased by upper class parents for their sons, this "son of an humble farmer," as he described himself, had bought his own commission as ensign, even though it meant running into debt. (His debts kept piling up and remained a burden until he was an old man.) He had been born in southern Ireland in 1780. At the age of eleven he left school to help his father on the farm. As a boy, he heard people talking about the French Revolution and the spectacular rise of Napoleon Bonaparte on the continent. When a Yeomanry Corps (comparable to the Canadian militia) was formed in Ireland, James enlisted, though not yet sixteen. From the beginning he showed exceptional talent and at seventeen was promoted to sergeant over the heads of his father and older brother.

Not surprisingly, James' next step was to enlist in the regular army, and in 1799 he was drafted as sergeant to the 49th Regiment in England. There the nineteen-year-old boy came under a young British Officer who was to have a great influence on his life — Lieutenant-Colonel Isaac Brock.

One day, when Sergeant FitzGibbon was taking dictation from Colonel Brock, repeating the last word of each sentence after him, he mispronounced the word "ascertain." Rebuked by Brock, James became ashamed of his ignorance. He resolved to improve himself and bought a spelling-book, a dictionary and a grammar "and from that hour I made every effort to educate myself," he said. He succeeded remarkably well.

FitzGibbon showed courage and determination in battle, but above all, he quickly learned how to get on with his men. He describes the occasion which taught him his first basic lesson in psychology:

> One morning, at early drill, everything went amiss with me. I became angry, scolded, and even used my cane, which was then allowed, and, in fact, was too much used. At length I let the men stand at ease, and walked about in front, thinking what could be the cause of the want of my usual success; when, fortunately, it occurred to me that it must be owing to my own impatient and angry temper.
>
> At once I began to speak gently to the men, and promised to shorten the time of drill by half an hour, if they exerted themselves; after which all went well. . . . After some time, an idea occurred to me that I should treat the men as a lady would her piano — that is, put them in tune (good humor) before I played upon them; and thus I soon ascertained that I could readily lead nine men where I could not drive one.*

Sergeant FitzGibbon first saw action in Holland against Napoleon's army, at Egmond-op-Zee, where he was captured but was soon released in an exchange of prisoners. Two years later he participated in the Battle of Copenhagen. Then his regiment was transferred to Quebec, and in June, 1802, James FitzGibbon, now sergeant-major, saw for the first time the land that would be his own for the next forty-five years. On Colonel Brock's recommendation, he obtained his ensign's commission in 1806 and was promoted to a lieutenancy in 1809.

Brock gave FitzGibbon assignments that required

*H. J. Morgan, *Sketches of Celebrated Canadians* (Quebec, Hunter, 1862) , pp. 194-5.

courage and endurance. In 1812 FitzGibbon escorted a brigade of twenty-four small boats "laden with Ordinance Stores of great importance to the Posts in the Upper Province," from Montreal to Kingston, passing through the dangerous rapids in the St. Lawrence, and proceeding up river in full view of the American shore. Some Americans at Ogdensburg planned to intercept his boats at Toussaint's Island, but one of the islanders escaped to the Canadian shore and warned the militia. The Canadians fired on the American gunboat and succeeded in thwarting the attack.

The following winter FitzGibbon conducted a brigade of forty-five sleighs carrying military stores, from Kingston to Niagara, a distance of 250 miles. Winter was the best time for travel in those days of bumpy and muddy pioneer roads. The frost froze the mud and the snow smoothed out the bumps, but as FitzGibbon's men drove their horses around the shores of the Bay of Quinte and Lake Ontario, they were exposed day after day to the biting January winds blowing across the ice-cold lake. Who is there today who would want to undertake such a journey?

The dauntless Irish officer was discouraged, and even disgusted, when the British failed to follow up the American retreat to Fort George after the Battle of Stoney Creek, but he grasped the initiative by gaining permission to organize his own guerilla unit. He divided his fifty men into three groups for greater mobility in the woods and ravines, and to confuse the enemy as to how many of them there were. Instead of the usual bugle calls, it is said that the men rang their signals with cow-bells. According to tradition FitzGibbon's men were called the "Green Tigers." This was actually the nickname for the entire 49th Regiment, which was noted for its daring and was distinguished by the green facings on the men's tunics. W. Hamilton Merritt said that FitzGibbon's detachment was sometimes called the "Irish Greens" or "bloody boys" and that they occasionally wore green jackets as a disguise.

The location of De Cew's house served well for scouting and guerilla activities. Set on a height of land, the house was surrounded by wooded ravines and streams. Hiding-places were plentiful and tall trees could be used for making observations. The men were determined to stop the raiding parties that had been terrorizing the settlers, robbing them and taking able-bodied men such as John De Cew prisoner. The chief villain in this war game was Captain Cyrenius Chapin, a Buffalo doctor, who, like FitzGibbon, commanded a small troop of his own men. Just as an army of today speaks of "liberating" the people of an enemy country, so Chapin claimed he was "protecting the inhabitants [of Upper Canada] from the outrages of the enemy [the British] and their property from the merciless plunderers." His main purpose was to clear the frontier of "persons inimical to the States." Except for a few American sympathizers who co-operated with Chapin, the Canadian settlers did not appreciate his efforts to "protect" them. They despised him and called him a brigand.

Chapin and his mounted "vagabonds" were Fitz-Gibbon's prime targets. One day FitzGibbon discovered that Chapin and his men were on their way to Chippawa and he determined to waylay them on Lundy's Lane, now a leading east-west street in Niagara Falls. Leaving his own men hidden in the woods at Drummond Hill (where Drummond Road of today intersects Lundy's Lane), FitzGibbon rode on ahead to reconnoitre. Near Deffield's Inn on the Portage Road (now Main Street) at Lundy's

Lane, a woman by the name of Kerby ran out to warn him that Captain Chapin had just passed by with a hundred or more soldiers in addition to his own mounted riflemen. She had seen them go into a nearby house, apparently making a search, and she thought they might soon return. FitzGibbon was not deterred. He noticed a single cavalry horse standing by the inn, and assuming it belonged to one of Chapin's men, he dismounted and went inside. He found not one but two Americans there — a rifleman and a soldier. This is how Merritt described what happened.

> The former presented his piece on his entering the door. Fitz, without answering, gave him his hand, claiming an old acquaintance, which threw the man off his guard (he had likewise a green coat on, as had all his men at times . . .), with the other seized his gun. The soldier was in the act of firing when he fortunately caught his gun, brought both of them under his arm, by which means the muzzles of each were pointing at his comrade, both cocked, the friction of the two enabled him to keep them so firm that they could not with every exertion break his grasp. In this position he pulled and pushed them both out of the house, the steps of which were two or three feet high, he swearing and demanding them to surrender, they retorting the demand on him. Two or three inhabitants were standing by at the time and refused to assist him. Mrs. K. begged and threatened them to no effect. A small boy of Doct. Flemming's threw brickbats at them, done everything in his power. After a short struggle the rifleman drew Fitz's sword from its sheath with his left hand and was in the act of thrusting it in his breast when the woman of the house, Mrs. Deffield, who was standing in the door with

46

her child in her arms, kicked it out of his hand. He stooped [and] recovered it, she threw the child on the floor, ran out and wrenched it completely from him and hid it in the house. A few moments after her husband came up, knocked the flint out of one of the guns and disarmed the man. The other Fitz threw against the steps and disarmed him. [He] mounted his horse, led the other and drove the two gentlemen before him to his party. He had not left the place two minutes before the [American] party returned. Upon the whole it was a most gallant, daring and miraculous proceeding.

FitzGibbon, when recollecting the incident himself many years later, was perhaps more realistic than Merritt. He said it had "made a great noise in the Province much more than it deserved, running the round of the Newspapers in both Provinces, while, in fact, I acted indiscreetly by exposing myself and deserved blame." Indiscreet or not, people applauded the spunky action of the "Green Tiger." Chapin, for his part, resolved to get rid of this impudent foe. He persuaded his superior officers that it would be easy to wipe out FitzGibbon's post.

One day Captain Chapin (he called himself "Major") went to see Lieutenant-Colonel Charles Boerstler, an American officer stationed at Fort George. When Boerstler described the visit later, he said Chapin "talked largely about having scoured all the country with his forty followers, that he had been to the Beaver Dams, that the enemy had fortified Decoo's stone house, that there were one company of regulars and from sixty to one hundred Indians at that post, that if this stronghold was destroyed the enemy could no longer show himself in this quarter; that five hundred men with a couple of field pieces could effect this. . . ."

Boerstler was not impressed. He considered Chapin "a vain boasting liar" and even doubted his loyalty. He listened to Chapin's plan "with indifference and dismissed [him] with coolness."

But a shock was in store for Colonel Boerstler. That very afternoon (June 23) he received orders from Brigadier-General John P. Boyd that he was to lead 500 men against De Cews' house "to capture or dislodge the enemy and batter down" the house. Boerstler, like a good soldier, swallowed his disapproval and said, "Very well, Sir, when do I march?" The answer was, "This evening."

As events proved, Colonel Boerstler was a better judge of the situation than General Boyd or Captain Chapin. Boyd was even more of an adventurer than Chapin. He had been a "soldier of fortune" in India where he had sold his services to several Indian princes in turn. One of his fellow officers in the War of 1812 described Boyd as "a compound of ignorance, vanity and petulance" whose bravery in battle was "vapouring" and "boisterous." Unfortunately for the Americans of the 14th Regiment, General Boyd was in command that June of 1813. He accepted Chapin's plan of attack and ordered Boerstler to take his 500 men to Queenston on the evening of June 23, and proceed to De Cew's house the next day. Chapin would act as guide.

The plan sounded simple, and as far as Chapin was concerned, FitzGibbon was "in the bag." Little did he realize that he would be outwitted by a woman.

Even today we cannot be sure how Laura Secord learned of the American plan. It is a secret she and her husband kept to themselves, perhaps for fear of reprisals. In a letter she wrote some forty years after the event, Laura said simply, "It was while the

48

Americans had possession of the frontier, that I learned the plans of the American commander. . . ." Later still, in a memorial she prepared in 1860, Laura stated that ". . . living on the Frontier during the whole of the war I had frequent opportunities of knowing the moves of the American forces. I thus was enabled to obtain important information which I deemed proper to communicate to the British Commander Col. FitzGibbon, then Lieut. FitzGibbon of the 49th Regt. . . ."

Mrs. Secord was an old lady when she made these statements. What had she told her children while the incident was fresh in her memory? Her son Charles gave his version in a letter he wrote in 1845 to a periodical called *The Church*. He said, "My mother, living on the frontier the whole of the late American war, a warm supporter of the British cause, frequently met with the American officers and . . . overheard an American officer say to other of the officers that they intended to surprise and capture the British troops at the Beaver Dam."

The early biographers of Mrs. Secord concluded that American troops had either been billeted in the Secord house, or had gone there for meals. Mrs. Emma Currie in her generally reliable *Story of Laura Secord* went so far as to say that on the twenty-third of June, Colonel Boerstler dined at the Secord house in Queenston with some fellow officers who were billeted there, and that "they talked freely of their plans." We know now that Boerstler was not at Laura Secord's house that day because he did not arrive at Queenston until late that evening.

Tradition is strong in the Secord family that American officers dined in the Secord home and that Laura overheard the conversation. A granddaughter, Laura Secord Clark, related the story as

49

she recalled her grandmother having told it to her as a child:

> She told me that the Americans had come into the house and asked her for something to eat, and Grandmother said to the black servants, "Put everything you have got on the table because we cannot resist them," and amongst other things they put some liquor on.
>
> She listened outside the window where they were taking their supper and she overheard them say that they would surprise Colonel FitzGibbon at Beaver Dam.*

The two narratives as told by Charles Secord and Laura's granddaughter correspond. Moreover there is good reason to believe that Captain Chapin (not Boerstler) may have called at the Secord home to demand a meal.

It is known that Chapin was in Queenston a few days before the Battle of Beaver Dams. The *Buffalo Gazette* of June 29, 1813, carried this news item: "On Saturday week (19th June), the mounted men under Major Chapin passed down to Queenston. . . ." Then follows an account of two episodes in which Chapin's men were engaged, the last being on Monday, June 21, when "N. D. Keep, belonging to Major Chapin's corps, was taken asleep by the enemy. . . . The party returned to Queenston."

We can now imagine what took place when Chapin returned to Queenston with some of his men after suffering the humiliation of having a man captured, the third within a few days. Knocking on the Secord door, Chapin demanded a meal for himself and his men. The women hastily spread supper

---

*"The Story of Laura Ingersoll Secord, wife of Captain James Secord as related by Laura Secord Clark, Granddaughter of Laura Secord to Mrs. George S. Henry." Ontario Dept. of Public Records and Archives, Misc., 1933.

on the family table in the large kitchen and then withdrew. Left to themselves, the men, sitting around the table, talked as they ate. Chapin, still smarting from FitzGibbon's triumphs over him, began boasting of the plan he knew was in the making — how the Americans would march to De Cew's, destroy FitzGibbon's headquarters and take the whole detachment captive. Laura, who had slipped quietly around to the back of the house, heard Chapin's excited voice through the open window.

The men soon finished their meal and, noisily pushing back their chairs, strode out of the house, mounted their horses and rode off to their quarters at Fort George. Laura Secord hastened to tell her husband what she had heard. Her granddaughter takes up the story.

'James, somebody ought to tell Colonel FitzGibbon they are coming.' Grandfather said, 'Well if I crawled on my hands and knees, I could not get there in time.' She said, 'Well, suppose I go?' He said 'You go, with the country in so disturbed a state? I do not think any man could get through, let alone a woman.' Grandmother said 'You forget James that God will take care of me.'

5/HOW
LAURA WARNED
FITZGIBBON

There was no time to waste. James and Laura hastily made their plans. They decided that Laura would leave early the next morning. First she would go to St. David's to see her half-brother Charles Ingersoll who was sick in bed with a fever at Hannah Secord's (Stephen Secord's widow). Charles was engaged to be married to Hannah's eldest daughter, twenty-year-old Elizabeth. The call at St. David's would serve a double purpose. A visit to her sick brother would serve as a good excuse to offer if American sentries questioned Laura about where she was going. Then there was the chance that Charles would be sufficiently recovered to take the message to FitzGibbon, or perhaps one of Hannah's boys could go.

Dawn came around 4:30 *a.m.* (it was long before daylight saving had ever been thought of) and Laura rose with the sun. Slipping into the girls' room, she told them she was going to see Uncle Charles; she didn't know when she would be back, but they were to look after the little children until she came. Harriet, who was about seven at the time, recalled years later, "I remember seeing my mother leave the house on that fateful morning, but neither I nor my sisters knew on what errand she was bent."

At that early hour there was a cool breeze but the air was damp after an all-night rain, and the day promised to be sultry. Emerging from the back door of the house, Laura walked briskly along the familiar road to St. David's. Clad in a house-dress she had made herself, of brown cotton print with an all-over design of little orange flowers, Laura felt comfortably cool. The long, straight skirt, gathered at the back, hung down almost to the ground from the high waist-line of her dress. The sleeves came just below the elbows. Around her neck, Laura wore a white muslin kerchief, and on her head, a white cotton bonnet as was the fashion of the day. Surprising as it may seem, Laura did not have on comfortable walking shoes. Except for moccasins which many country women wore outdoors, there were then no walking shoes such as women have today. Laura wore house slippers, probably made of light kid with low heels and with ties at the instep. They offered very poor protection on country roads, still less in crossing fields or going through the woods. But Laura was used to walking in her slippers and she made her way quickly along the road. In less than an hour she was in St. David's, going down the lane past the Secord mill to Hannah's stone house.

Just a minute, you say, what about the cow? And the American sentry? The truth is, there was no cow and probably no American sentry either, though Laura certainly expected to encounter a sentry. "I found I should have great difficulty in getting through the American guards which were ten miles out in the country," she wrote forty years later. Did she think the guards were ten miles from Queenston or from Fort George? We do not know, but according to an American "statement of facts" made public after the war, the American pickets were no farther than two miles from Fort George. So Laura was in no danger from them. She had no way of knowing this, however, and the fact does not detract in the slightest from the courage she showed in exposing herself, as she thought, to the risk of being stopped by enemy guards.

As to the cow, neither Laura herself, nor any member of her family, ever mentioned one. Her great-niece, Mrs. Elizabeth Ann Gregory (a granddaughter of Mrs. Stephen Secord) stated flatly that "the cow and the milk-pail are a fable." It appears that the "fable" was the invention of William F. Coffin who, in 1864, wrote a book called *1812; the War and Its Moral.** He pictured Laura having difficulty with "the American advanced sentry," and milking a cow in his presence, which she then drove before her into the woods. Although the Secords may very well have had a cow (many villagers kept cows), there is no evidence that Laura was accompanied by one on any part of her walk to Beaver Dams.

Let us return to Laura as she knocked on the door of Hannah Secord's house in St. David's. A surprised Hannah opened the door.

Laura's first words were to ask about Charles. Her heart sank when she heard he was still sick in bed. She sat down to rest as she told Hannah and the pale, delicate Elizabeth about the secret plan to capture FitzGibbon and her anxiety to get word to him. If she had hoped that her journey might end at St. David's, she realized now that this would be impossible. Charles could not get out of bed, and Hannah's two older sons, James and David, were with the militia. Twelve-year-old Alex was home at the time and, when an old man, he recorded his recollection of his aunt's visit that morning. Laura

*Montreal, Lovell, 1864.

54

stuck to her determination to take the message herself, and her niece, Elizabeth Secord, offered to accompany her.

In order to avoid encounters with American soldiers on the direct road to Beaver Dams (a distance of about ten miles), the women decided to take the longer way by Shipman's Corners (now a busy five-corners shopping area at the intersection of Highway No. 8 and the old Welland Canal in St. Catharines). This would bring them into British-held territory and they may also have thought there would be a chance of meeeting Captain Merritt whose home was at Twelve Mile Creek (St. Catharines). They knew he would ride galloping to Beaver Dams with the message once he heard of the plot.

It was still early in the morning, perhaps around 8 o'clock, when Laura and Elizabeth set out. They took the black swamp road to Shipman's Corners. It led them through soggy swamps and woods and along a dirt road made muddy from the previous night's rain. One can imagine how the mosquitoes must have pestered them. The day grew increasingly hot and humid as the June sun rose higher in the sky. The two women had to pause often to rest and get their breath. Their light slippers kept coming off in the mud. Elizabeth's feet became blistered and she felt exhausted. By the time they came to the bridge over the creek near Shipman's Corners, Elizabeth could see that she was holding her aunt back. She was far from strong and, indeed, had only one more year to live. She never became Charles Ingersoll's wife.

Although Laura had walked farther than Elizabeth that morning, and, like her, was hot and tired, she had no intention of turning back. In spite of her delicate build she was wiry and very determined. Bidding her niece good-bye, she continued on her journey alone. It is believed that Elizabeth remained with friends at Shipman's Corners.

From here on, Laura was uncertain of the way, and afraid of encountering unfriendly Indians. Mrs. Gregory, who was born after the war and lived with her grandmother until her marriage, said, "I remember well of sitting in childish astonishment and terror, listening to Aunt [Laura Secord] and Grandma [Hannah Secord] talking over the affair, and of hearing her relate the fears she entertained of meeting and being taken prisoner by the American Indians before she had reached the British lines."

Laura could not be sure the British had a firm hold on the territory she was in, and she avoided the main roads in making her way to De Cew's place from Shipman's. Following the general direction of Twelve Mile Creek, she crossed over fields and went through woods. In addition to her fear of Indians, Laura must have had qualms about the wild animals that dwelt in the forest — of wildcats that pounced on their prey from trees, of wolves that were still common. Even in the fields, there was the danger of rattle-snakes. They were plentiful in the Niagara Peninsula. (John De Cew told how the rattle-snakes came into his original log house in such numbers before he had the floor laid and door put in, that he had to sleep in a hammock slung from the rafters.)

Tradition has it that Laura lost her slippers in the course of the day, and it would indeed have been surprising if she had not, considering the soft ground in the woods and the inadequacy of her slippers. It was evening before she came to De Cew Falls, and she knew she was now approaching De Cew's house. "When I came to a field belonging to a Mr. De Cou, in the neighbourhood of the Beaver

56

Dams, I then had walked nineteen miles," Mrs. Secord recalled in a letter to the American historian, Benson Lossing, many years later. "By that time daylight had left me. I yet had a swift stream of water [Twelve Mile Creek] to cross over an old fallen tree, and to climb a high hill, which fatigued me very much."

Those who question why it took Laura a whole day to walk nineteen or twenty miles, need only compare her achievement with that of some of today's youth who walk a similar distance in the annual "Miles for Millions" walks. These young people have the advantage of rest-stops for food and first-aid, and their way leads over paved roads or well-trodden paths, with a minimum of hills. Laura Secord, by contrast, walked over muddy roads and through tangled thickets that caught on her skirts; and she had steep hills to climb when she was most fatigued on the last part of her journey. She had little food with her and there was no place to get coffee or tea. She may have eaten something at St. David's and perhaps she had taken a sandwich with her. Berries would be available as she went along, and there would be fresh water in springs. But when her feet became blistered there was no basin of hot water in which to bathe them, and no band-aids to protect them. The hot, sticky day was the worst kind for walking. Only a woman used to a rugged life and of resolute will could have endured the pain and fatigue of such a journey.

As twilight deepened, Laura was near exhaustion but she was cheered by the thought of soon seeing De Cew's house high on the ridge. Then, suddenly she found herself surrounded by the dreaded Indians. She had stumbled on the encampment of Indian reinforcements who had arrived only a day or so previously. Let Laura tell the story:

Upon advancing to the Indians they all rose and with some yells said "Woman," which made me tremble. I cannot express the awful feeling it gave me, but I did not lose my presence of mind. I was determined to persevere. I went up to one of the chiefs, made him understand that I had great news for Capt. Fitzgibbon, and that he must let me pass to his camp, or that he and his party would be all taken. The chief at first objected to let me pass, but finally consented, after some hesitation, to go with me and accompany me to Fitzgibbon's station, which was at the Beaver Dam, where I had an interview with him. I then told him what I had come for, and what I had heard — that the Americans intended to make an attack upon the troops under his command, and would, from their superior numbers capture them all.

FitzGibbon looked at her in amazement. He had never seen this woman before and knew nothing about her, but he was impressed by her earnestness. Her face was drawn with fatigue and flushed from the heat. Her deep-set eyes had dark circles under them and were full of anxiety. Her long dress was torn and bedraggled from her walk through the bush, and she was without her slippers. Convinced that she was telling the truth, FitzGibbon directed some of his men to escort her to safety at the neighbouring Turney farm.

Writing of the incident in later years, FitzGibbon said, "Mrs. Secord was a person of slight and delicate frame and made this effort in weather excessively warm, and I dreaded at the time that she must suffer in health in consequence of fatigue and anxiety, she having been exposed to danger from the enemy, through whose line of communication she had to pass."

When Laura returned home to her anxious family, the day after the battle, she was "exhausted and fatigued." Looking back years afterwards she wondered "how I could have gone through so much fatigue with the fortitude to accomplish it."

To what avail had she made this great effort? The Battle of Beaver Dams would show.

6/VICTORY
AT BEAVER
DAMS

After Mrs. Secord had left him, FitzGibbon thought quickly. She had said the Americans would probably leave Fort George the next morning (June 23). That meant the attack might come tomorrow. The first thing was to notify Colonel Bisshopp of the warning. He was stationed, as has been mentioned, at Twenty Mile Creek near the southern shore of Lake Ontario, and approximately twenty miles west of the American base at Fort George. Midway between, was Major De Haren's outpost near present-day St. Catharines. FitzGibbon's own unit at De Cew's was on the old Mountain Road leading from St. David's, and was seven miles south of De Haren's.

It would take time for Bisshopp and De Haren to act in response to FitzGibbon's message, but the Irish Green lieutenant was not one to sit around and wait. Although he had only fifty men in his detachment, over 400 Indians were encamped at Beaver Dams, less than two miles east of De Cew's house. ("Beaver Dams" referred to an expanse of beaver meadows and dams, as well as to a small settlement north of the present community of Beaverdams.) The Indians had arrived only two days before. There were 180 Caughnawagas and others from

Lower Canada (Quebec) under the militia captain, Dominique Ducharme; 200 of the Six Nations Indians from Brantford, Upper Canada, led by Captain William Johnson Kerr, son-in-law of the late Chief Joseph Brant; and some seventy from other parts of Upper Canada.

As a precaution, FitzGibbon said, "I placed the Indians . . . together with my own Detachment in a Situation to intercept the American Detachment, and we occupied it during the night of the 22d." But the Americans did not come that night.

The next morning, Captain Ducharme went on a scouting expedition to the Niagara River with twenty-five of his Indians. He saw no sign of the advancing army. He reported, however, that "We discovered a barge filled with soldiers; the Indians fired upon it, killed four men and made seven prisoners. As we were within sight of Fort George I ordered my Indians to hurry away their prisoners. The American cavalry pursued us, and two young Iroquois, having remained behind, as they stated to capture horses, one of them was made a prisoner."

This was a typical incident in the incessant border warfare on the Niagara frontier, but it was unrelated to the battle that was shaping up. Not until the evening of that same day (the twenty-third) did Colonel Boerstler set out from Fort George with his 500 men to march the six miles south to Queenston. They arrived about 11 *p.m.* taking great pains to prevent word of their arrival from reaching the British. "Patrols and pickets were immediately sent out to prevent citizens from escaping to give intelligence. No candles were suffered to be lighted and officers and men laid down on their arms," Boerstler reported.

Between seven and eight the next morning (June 24), the Indian scouts who had been sent out from

Beaver Dams to reconnoitre, saw the American troops advancing. They rushed back to camp "giving the death-cry" — a warning that an enemy attack was on the way. Ducharme notified his superior officer, Major De Haren, and got permission to place his Indians in the woods rather than in the regular formation for attack. The spot chosen was a beechwoods near the junction of the old Mountain Road that ran along the escarpment, and the north-south road from Twelve Mile Creek, on the edge of present-day Thorold. The Indians took up their positions on both sides of the road, hidden in the woods. Captain Kerr was in command. Lieutenant FitzGibbon stood by, on "an eminence to the right" of the Mountain Road.

Unaware that a trap had been laid, the Americans marched on toward De Cew's. The men were becoming tired after their long tramp over hills and valleys. They had not been allowed any break in their journey, and the morning air, which had seemed cool and fresh at first, had become increasingly warm and humid.

A detached observer would have seen a colourful procession. In the vanguard, were the mounted militiamen in their gray uniforms, led by Captain Cyrenius Chapin, the "guide" of the expedition. (He proved to be a very poor guide. No sooner had the Americans left St. David's than they discovered that Chapin did not know the road. Colonel Boerstler had to seek directions from inhabitants, and he compelled one of them to act as guide). Immediately following the militia, rode Colonel Boerstler on his horse, leading his 300 foot soldiers of the 14th Regiment, their blue cockaded hats and blue jackets reflecting the blue of the summer sky, their white trousers standing out against the brown of the dirt road and the deep green of the wooded hillside. Behind the infantry marched the artillery. Two four-horse teams hauled the wagons laden with some 5,000 rounds of ammunition. Other teams attached to two-wheeled limbers pulled the field guns — a 12-pounder and a 6-pounder. Then came another hundred soldiers of the 6th and 23rd Regiments, led by Major Taylor. Finally, bringing up the rear, were some twenty cavalrymen, the brass fittings of their harness catching the morning sunlight. Flankers rode to right and left of the troops.

When the detachment entered the beechwoods, those in advance could see the open fields before them. They knew they were within two or three miles of their objective. But suddenly shots rang out. Some of the rear guard of cavalry fell dead from their horses. Indians crossed the road behind the troops, and the woods rang with shots from their guns. The Americans, who had been counting on surprising the British, were themselves taken by surprise. Caught in an ambush, they were forced to fight at both front and rear. They had been trained to do battle in orderly lines, and had no experience dealing with an enemy hidden in the woods. "The enemy's balls reached us from every direction, while he was concealed," Boerstler reported the next day to the American commander, General Henry Dearborn. The hard-pressed soldiers imagined the Indians to be more numerous than they actually were. They had heard stories of the scalping of the wounded by Indian braves, and were terrified lest this fate awaited them.

Major Taylor's horse fell from under him. Colonel Boerstler was wounded in the thigh shortly after the battle began. Both officers showed great courage. Boerstler continued to ride his horse and give commands although in great pain. He tried to drive the Indians into the open field and partially succeeded on his right, only to be attacked furiously by the Indians on his left. No matter what action the Americans took, the Indians kept up a constant fire from the woods.

The boastful Captain Chapin, who had got the Americans into this mess, disappeared and was discovered hiding in a hollow alongside the ammunition wagons which had been moved some distance to the rear out of reach of the Indians' fire. Boerstler was furious. He dashed to the rear and said to Chapin, "For God's sake, Major, do something. If you do not fight your men then take them and furnish mine with ammunition and carry off the wounded to the wagons, that I may not be compelled to take men for this purpose out of my ranks." Captain Chapin hauled a keg of cartridges on his horse and handed it to a soldier. Then he resumed his shelter in the hollow.

Colonel Boerstler was forced to detach a man from each of his companies to carry off the wounded, place them on the wagons and move them to a protected position some distance away. The situation was now desperate. The colonel resolved to make one last charge to clear the road, and then begin a retreat. But it would be against great odds. Even if he could get the road cleared, the distance to Fort George was seventeen miles. No provision had been made for reinforcements and the troops were now reduced by some 80 killed or wounded. Those who remained were exhausted from the three-hour battle after their long and wearying march in the heat. Boerstler himself was suffering from his wound. Most ominous of all, the ammunition was running low. Boerstler knew that the British had regular troops in reserve who had not yet been engaged in the battle.

At this critical point, Lieutenant FitzGibbon rode up. Sizing up the situation, he decided by a *ruse de guerre* to bluff the Americans into surrender. With a white handkerchief hoisted, and bugles sounding the "cease firing," FitzGibbon offered to negotiate. Boerstler sent Captain Andrew McDowell to talk to him. FitzGibbon told McDowell that he had been sent by Major De Haren to demand surrender. British reinforcements had arrived, he said, and the Americans were greatly outnumbered. Furthermore, he went on, some Indians fom the Northwest had come who would be much harder to control than those who had been fighting. He feared a massacre would result if the Americans held out. He offered to let an American officer view the British troops to see for himself how many there were. His offer was accepted, but when the American officer went to the head of the lane where the British detachment was waiting, Captain John Hall refused to let him see his troops, saying this would be too humiliating. (Actually Hall had only a small force of dragoons with him as the main force under De Haren had not yet arrived.)

Colonel Boerstler conferred with his officers. Should they surrender or run the risk of a bloody retreat? The officers agreed that surrender would be the more humane course to take. Boerstler then sent Captain McDowell back to FitzGibbon to obtain the best terms he could. Thus it came about that 462 American soldiers including 22 officers surrendered themselves and their two field guns and wagons, to Lieutenant James FitzGibbon and his fifty men.

Major De Haren arrived on the scene in time to sign the capitulation papers along with Captain McDowell, and De Haren officially received the surrender. Under the terms, Colonel Boerstler and his troops became prisoners of war; the officers were to retain their arms, horses and baggage; the militia and volunteers were to be allowed to return to the United States on parole. Captain Chapin, leader of the militia, claimed afterwards that the last part of the agreement was not kept. He said the militiamen were held prisoners at Burlington Heights. When they were being transported by boat to Kingston three weeks later, Chapin and some of his men overpowered the guards, gained possession of the boats, changed course for Fort George, and thus effected their escape.

The Indians were bitterly disappointed that after fighting the battle, they did not get credit for winning the victory. In his official report, Colonel Bisshopp was indeed quite just. He said, "In this affair the Indian warriors under the Command of Captain Kerr were the only Force actually engaged; to them great merit is due, and to them I feel particularly obliged for their gallant conduct on this occasion." But of course the Indians did not see Bisshopp's report, and the public acclaim went to Lieutenant James FitzGibbon, "through whose address the Capitulation was entered into," as Bisshopp said, and to whose conduct "may be attributed the surrender of the American Army." Colonel Bisshopp also praised Major De Haren "for his speedy movement to the point of attack and execution of the arrangements I had previously made with him."

The Montreal *Gazette* reported the battle in glowing terms in its issue of July 6, 1813:

> . . . we have much satisfaction in communicating to the public the particulars of a campaign not of a *General* with his *thousands* but of a *lieutenant* with his *tens* only. The manner in which a bloodless victory was obtained by a force so comparatively and almost incredibly small with that

of the enemy, the cool determination and the hardy presence of mind evinced by this highly meritorious officer in conducting the operations incident to the critical situation in which he was placed with his little band of heroes, and the brilliant result which crowned those exertions will, while they make known to the world the name of Lieutenant FitzGibbon, reflect new lustre, if possible, on the well earned reputation of the gallant 49th Regt., and class the event with the most extraordinary occurrences of the present accursed war.

The Indian viewpoint was expressed sardonically by Lieutenant John Norton whom W. H. Merritt quoted as saying, "The Cognawagas Indians fought the Battle; the Mohawks or Six Nations got the plunder, and Lieutenant FitzGibbon got the Credit." As to the plunder, a Buffalo paper stated that after the surrender some of the Indians robbed the officers of their side arms and stripped the soldiers of some articles of clothing. Merritt said that the Caughnawagas were so displeased about their unfair treatment that they returned home to Lower Canada in a few days. Their leader, Captain Dominique Ducharme, had a special grievance against the Mohawks. He complained that in the midst of the fighting, most of them had abandoned his Indians; that Captain Kerr and Lieutenant John Brant had gone to bring them back, but had then themselves disappeared for the remainder of the battle.

It was Captain Kerr, however, who persisted in getting recognition for the Indians. He was a bold and determined man who later became wealthy and prominent in public life. He was elected to the Legislative Assembly in Upper Canada in 1820, became superintendent of the Burlington Canal, and achieved notoriety in 1832 for an alleged attempt on the life of William Lyon Mackenzie. Nearly eight years after the Battle of Beaver Dams, Kerr addressed a memorial to the Duke of York as "Field Marshal and Commander-in-Chief of all His Majesty's land forces." He asked for a pension and, in support of his claim, he outlined his war services, stressing the part he had played as commander of the Indians at Beaver Dams, and enclosing testimonials from three British officers. One was from Captain James FitzGibbon who said, "With respect to the affair with Captain Boerstler, not a shot was fired on our side by any but the Indians. They beat the American Detachment into a state of Terror, and the only share I claim is the taking advantage of a favourable moment to offer them protection from the Tomahawk and the scalping knife: The Indian Department did all the rest!"

Apart from the question of who deserved the credit for the victory, what significance did the Battle of Beaver Dams have? Most assuredly it represented a serious reverse for the Americans. Coming so soon after the fiasco at Stoney Creek, it reflected discredit on the high command. Within two weeks, Major-General Henry Dearborn, the American commander of the frontier from Niagara to the Atlantic coast, was relieved of his command.

The Canadian historian, Dr. George F. G. Stanley, has pointed out that after the Battle of Beaver Dams, "The old fear of the Indians took possession of the American troops at Fort George and following Colonel Boerstler's disaster they did not venture to send a patrol more than a mile from the fort. . . ."* More significantly, Colonel G. W. L. Nicholson, the Canadian military historian, has stated that "With these two set-backs [Stoney Creek and Beaver Dams,] the Americans com-

---

*"The Indians in the War of 1812," *Canadian Historical Review*, XXXI (1950), p. 158.

pletely lost the initiative in the Niagara theatre. In December they abandoned Fort George and burned Newark; and before 1813 ended, British regulars had carried the war across the Niagara River, capturing Fort Niagara and putting Lewiston and Buffalo to the torch."**

We may also speculate on what would have happened if the Americans had succeeded in capturing FitzGibbon and his men, and destroying De Cew's house with its store of ammunition and supplies. No doubt they would have followed up the victory by attacking the British strongholds on the south side of Lake Ontario. The Americans, rather than the British would have had the initiative on the Niagara frontier, with what results no one can say.

Colonel Charles Boerstler was severely criticized in the United States for surrendering to the British. In his words "slander and misrepresentation . . . [assailed] my conduct in regard to the 'battle of the Beaver Dams.' " A court of inquiry into his conduct met in Baltimore early in 1815. After hearing the evidence the court concluded unanimously "That the personal deportment of lieut. col. Boerstler . . . was that of a brave, zealous and deliberate officer, and the conduct of the *regular* officers and men under his command, was equally honorable to themselves and to their country." The emphasis on "regular officers" was apparently aimed at Captain Chapin, a militia officer, whose information leading to the attack "proved to have been erroneous." The court stated that "the surrender was justified by existing circumstances," and concluded pointedly "that the misfortune of the day is not to be ascribed to lieut. col. Boerstler, or the detachment under his command."

**G. W. L. Nicholson, *The Gunners of Canada* (Toronto, McClelland and Stewart, 1967), vol. 1, pp. 68-9.

7/THE
HEROINE IN
LIMBO

In the controversy about the Battle of Beaver Dams, no reference whatever was made to Laura Secord. FitzGibbon in his official report, written the day of the battle, said only, "At DeCou's this morning, about seven o'clock, I received information that about One thousand of the Enemy, with two Guns, were advancing towards me from St. Davids." His "information" was, of course, brought by Indian scouts as we know from Captain Dominique Ducharme's account, published in a Montreal newspaper: "On the 24th, I sent scouts out to different roads leading from Fort George. About 8 o'clock two returned announcing that the enemy was coming in large numbers — infantry, cavalry, wagons, etc. . . ."

The question has often been asked: Why did FitzGibbon not mention Mrs. Secord's warning in his report? Did he omit it deliberately so that the full glory of Boerstler's surrender would fall on him? This is certainly a possibility. Like other self-made men, James FitzGibbon knew the value of self-promotion. At thirty-three, he was still only a lieutenant, and was ambitious for further advancement. The Indians, as we have seen, were angry that he had received the praise for the victory which they had won. FitzGibbon, in his turn, accused two of his commanders of trying to deprive him of the credit for the American surrender. Actually, he succeeded in obtaining both the credit and the promotion. Years later when he recounted the story of his life, he said, ". . . on the 24th [June, 1813] I achieved a service for which I was immediately promoted to a company in another regiment." This was the Glengarry Light Infantry Fencibles, to which he was transferred as captain on October 14, 1813. (He had cause to regret this later because the regiment was disbanded in 1816, and Captain FitzGibbon was reduced to half-pay. Eventually he became colonel in the York militia.)

In defence of FitzGibbon's slight to Laura Secord, it may be argued that publicity about her deed would have been highly dangerous for her and her family while the War of 1812 continued. True, but was FitzGibbon's official report "publicity"? As a military document, he knew it would be kept confidential. Quite possibly it never even occurred to FitzGibbon to mention Mrs. Secord in his report on the battle. He had previously informed his superior officer, Colonel Cecil Bisshopp, of the message she had brought, otherwise the latter would not have made "the arrangements" with Major De Haren, to which he referred in the report previously quoted.*

The British officers knew that they could rely on the co-operation of loyal Canadian citizens to assist them in any way possible. They knew that the wives of militiamen were glad to pass on any information they might pick up which would be of any value. Seen in this perspective, FitzGibbon may have accepted Laura Secord's service as an example of the patriotism common among the people. There

*See p. 66.

is another angle. It was not unusual for women to act as scouts in the War of 1812. "I went on to Hainers Hill and sent an old woman over to reconnoitre, and ascertain their numbers," W. H. Merritt recorded in his Journal of the 1813 campaign. "She was detained, but by an excellent strategem she got released. She told me their situation. . . ." Who this "old woman" was we shall never know. *Her* courageous act remains anonymous.

To give James FitzGibbon his due, he proved to be a good friend to Laura Secord in later years. In the meantime, far from being celebrated as a heroine, she sank into oblivion.

After the exhausting ordeal of her twenty-mile walk, Laura Secord was relieved and happy to be back home safe and sound in the bosom of her family. But she could not afford the luxury of talking about her experience. Her children probably thought she had spent the previous two or three days and nights at their aunt's at St. David's. Laura and her husband kept their own counsel. The few others who knew of her walk — Mrs. Stephen Secord, her daughter Elizabeth (who died before the war ended) Charles Ingersoll and the Turneys — had equal cause to fear, and therefore to avoid, reprisals. It was many years before Mrs. Secord's secret became public knowledge.

When the war came to an end in late 1814, the village of Queenston was a wreck, its wharves and warehouses badly damaged or destroyed, many shops and houses battered or burned. The Secord house had been spared but James said later that he had been "twice plundered" of his moveable property. His business was gone now and he was incapacitated. Three years after the war James sold six lots he owned in Queenston, no doubt because he required the money.

The government was slow in providing compensation for disabilities. Records show that in 1822, James Secord applied for compensation for his wounds. The Medical Board declared him "incapable of earning his livelihood in consequence of wounds received in action with the Enemy." The pension which eventually came to him was small — only £18 a year (less than $50.00) — and was not adequate to meet the needs of his growing family. Two girls, Laura and Hannah, were born after the war, Laura in 1815 and Hannah a year or two later. One wonders how the Secords managed to survive in the lean postwar years. Their seven children ranged in age from the baby, Hannah, to Mary, some seventeen years her senior.

Romance came to Mary soon after the war. In 1816, she married William Trumble, a surgeon with the 37th Regiment. They went to Ireland to live. Mary's husband was well-to-do but the marriage lasted little more than a dozen years, when Mr. Trumble died leaving his widow with two daughters, Elizabeth and Mary, an estate in Ireland, and a fair-sized pension.

The second Secord daughter, Charlotte, remained unmarried. Harriet, who, it will be recalled, remembered seeing her mother leave the house to go to Beaver Dams but did not know "on what errand she was bent," got married in 1824 to a lawyer, David William Smith of St. Catharines. They had three children — two daughters, Laura Louisa and Mary Augusta, and one son, William James. Like her sister Mary, Harriet was left a widow, in her case after eighteen years of marriage.

Appolonia, Laura's youngest child at the time of Beaver Dams, died at the age of eighteen. The two youngest girls both got married in 1833, Laura at eighteen and Hannah at sixteen or seventeen. Both

lost their husbands and remarried. Laura's first
husband was Captain John Poore, her second Dr.
William Clarke.* Hannah married Hawley Williams,
and then Edward Carthew of Guelph.

Charles Badeau, the only boy in the family (born
in 1809) was "bred to the law" as his father put it.
He became a barrister and notary public in Queenston. Charles married Margaret Ann Robins of
Kingston and they had a family of three — two
sons, James and Charles, and a daughter, Alicia.

Death was a fairly frequent visitor to the Secord
connection. In 1832, the cholera epidemic took
Laura's half-brother, Charles Ingersoll.

While these family changes were taking place,
James and Laura were struggling to provide a livelihood. In those days, many positions or other
rewards were granted through government patronage, and persons seeking such favours appealed
directly to the lieutenant-governor. In the decades
following the war, the Secords presented several
petitions to the government. These petitions tell a
story of poverty, and of the continuing battle James
and Laura waged to obtain recognition and just re-
compense for their war services.

The first petition of which we have a record, was
written by James on February 25, 1820, and was
addressed to Lieutenant-Governor Sir Peregrine
Maitland. James asked for a "licence of occupation"
of part of the military reserve at Queenston on
which there was a stone quarry. He supported his
request in these words:

> The Petition of James Secord, Senior, of the Vil-
> lage of Queenston, Esquire, Humbly Sheweth
>   That your Petitioner is one of the oldest in-
> habitants of this Province — has had numerous

---

*Sometimes spelled "Clark."

Relatives in the British army, is Brother-in-Law to the late Honorable Richard Cartwright — is a Captain in the 2nd Regiment of Lincoln Militia — was wounded in the battle of Queenston — and twice plundered of all his Moveable property. That his wife embraced an opportunity of rendering some service, at the risk of her life, in going thro the Enemies' Lines to communicate information to a Detachment of His Majesty's Troops at the Beaver Dam in the month of June 1813 . . . .

As far as is known, this is the first reference on any document to Laura Secord's heroic deed. The petition was treated as confidential, as was customary, and the public remained unaware of Laura's act. James was granted a lease of the stone quarry and he derived a small income from it.

About seven years later, James applied for "some situation which His Ex'cy Sir P. Maitland did not find it convenient to give him," according to a note written by a government official. Maitland suggested instead that Mrs. Secord might be placed in charge of Brock's monument at Queenston, when completed.

The reference was to the first Brock monument, a 135-foot column erected by the government of Upper Canada in the 1820s.*

On the twelfth anniversary of the Battle of Queenston Heights, the bodies of Sir Isaac Brock and Lieutenant-Colonel John Macdonnell were removed from Fort George and deposited, with impressive ceremony, in a vault at the base of the column. This was in October, 1824, but the monument was not completed for several years by which

*This monument was destroyed in 1840 by a gunpowder explosion said to be the work of a rebel "Patriot." The present monument dates from 1854.

time Sir Peregrine Maitland had been transferred to Nova Scotia, and Sir John Colborne had become Lieutenant-Governor of Upper Canada. Unlike Maitland, the new Lieutenant-Governor had no special interest in the Secords.

Maitland may have known the Secords personally. He had built an elegant twenty-two-room summer residence on his estate called "Stamford Park." The house stood on a height of land with a magnificent view, only a short distance from St. David's. In the note quoted above, the official (Chief Justice John Beverley Robinson) said that Maitland "had a favorable opinion of the character & claims of Mr. Secord and his wife." Before he left Upper Canada in 1828, Maitland responded to their claims by appointing James Registrar of the Niagara District Surrogate Court. James had previously written two urgent letters stressing his precarious financial position. In one of these he said that the sheriff of the Niagara District had stripped him of every article he possessed. "There is now no remedy for me but to be thrown upon the world penniless, lame and in ill health."

His appointment as Registrar of the Surrogate Court saved James and his wife from this unhappy fate, but the "emoluments were very small." The Secords were experiencing tough times. In a letter to Laura's sister, Mrs. Mira Hitchcock of Great Barrington, Massachusetts, James said in December, 1829: "With respect to our wordly affairs I am sorry to say we are not very prosperous. We make out to live and have clothing and food, but riches, my dear woman, it seems to me, is not for James Secord. . . ."

Laura was still hoping that Lieutenant-Governor Colborne would keep Maitland's promise to give her the care of Brock's monument, but she had begun to suspect, with good reason, that pressure was being applied by Colonel Thomas Clark to give the appointment to someone else — the widow of the late Robert Nichol. Colonel Clark was the sole remaining commissioner of three, all from the Niagara area, who had been responsible for erecting the monument. The others had been Thomas Dickson and Lieutenant-Colonel Robert Nichol.

Colonel Nichol had been a prosperous merchant before the war, during which he served as quarter-master-general of the Upper Canada militia. Afterwards he was elected to the Upper Canada Assembly where he became chairman of the Public Accounts Committee. At the time of his untimely death in 1824, he was Judge of the Surrogate Court of the Niagara District. One evening in May, during an unseasonable snowstorm, Colonel Nichol was returning to his home in Stamford when he lost his way. His horse and vehicle tumbled over the precipice at Queenston literally dashing him to pieces. After the horror of the accident had subsided, it was learned that this prominent citizen had left his wife and four children destitute. Nichol's estate was saddled with debt, and his militia pension stopped with his death. Colonel Clark wanted to help Mrs. Nichol by giving her the charge of Brock's monument with its perquisites.

There can be little doubt that Mrs. Nichol's need was greater than Mrs. Secord's. The widow and her four children were forced to live off the charity of friends. It was only natural, however, for Mrs. Secord to be more sensitive to her own problems than to Mrs. Nichol's, and she wrote persistently to Colborne, reminding him of Maitland's promise. Colborne refused to interfere. He accepted Clark's advice, and the key to the monument went to Mrs. Nichol in 1831.

Laura's disappointment rankled deeply. She wrote a tart letter to Colborne's secretary, Edward McMahon, flatly contradicting "Colonel Clark's Statement of *several objections*" to her appointment, and quoting Sir Peregrine Maitland as having said "*positively*" to Colonel Clark that "it was too late to think of Mrs. Nichol as I had pledged my word to Mrs. Secord that as soon as possible she should have the *key*." How Laura's dark eyes must have flashed as she wrote that letter.

A touching sidelight on this issue was discovered in the visitors' book of Brock's monument for September 1829. It bears the following signatures: Laura Secord, Queenston; Mrs. Ingersoll and Mary Ann Ingersoll, Oxford; Mary Trumble, Ireland; and Laura Louise Smith, St. Catharines. How proudly Laura Secord must have shown her family group around the monument, thinking that this was but a rehearsal for the many occasions on which she would act as guide for other visitors.

In James Secord's letter to his sister-in-law, already mentioned, he gives an intimate glimpse of his wife at this time. "Your sister Laura never had health better. She bears her age [54] most remarkably considering her former delicate state of body. We are, however, Mira, getting old and grey heads, and now and then a tremor of the body. . . ."

Although the Secords had cause to be disillusioned with the way government patronage worked, they continued to present petitions in the hope of improving their poverty-stricken condition. James asked for land as a reward for his wartime services appealing, as before, on the grounds of his great need. He put it this way: " . . . the events attendant on a State of Warfare on the Frontier, for three years, had a most injurious effect on his [the petitioner's] affairs, which in connection with other circumstances, and the effect of his wound, have brought him with a numerous family into very distressed circumstances." The Executive Council responded favourably to this petition without stipulating how much land should be granted.

In 1833 James Secord was promoted from Registrar to Judge of the Niagara District Surrogate Court — the same position Colonel Robert Nichol had held. It may seem surprising that a man untrained in law should become judge, but there is a simple explanation. There were not enough lawyers in Upper Canada to go around, so it was very common to elevate laymen to the role of judge, especially in the Surrogate Courts. These courts, then as now, had jurisdiction over the wills and estates of deceased persons.

Evidently James found his new position more prestigious than profitable, for in July, 1835 he resigned to become Collector of Customs at Chippawa. In this post, he received no salary but was entitled to fees on the goods passing through the port, plus a share of all the seizures he made. Being collector was an enviable position and over a dozen applicants had competed with James for the appointment. His income from fees ranged from around £100 to £150 or more a year. In one exceptionally fruitful year (1838), Secord collected over £157 in fees, a sum that was exceeded only at the ports of Toronto, Kingston and Oakville. With his pension of £18 a year, James had an income equivalent to $300-$400, which was considered fairly good in those days.

The years at Chippawa must have been among the most pleasant in the married life of the Secords. Although there were times of crisis, in general the threat of war with the United States had receded, the Secord children were grown up, and James had a position of some status in the community. The village was beautifully situated three miles above Niagara Falls at the confluence of the Niagara River and Chippawa Creek (now the Welland River). As was said previously, Chippawa had been an important trading centre at one extremity of the old Portage Road, and the first Welland Canal, opened in November, 1829, brought ships from Lake Ontario into Chippawa Creek, past the village of Chippawa and on to the Niagara River. (Later routes by-passed Chippawa and favoured the towns of Welland and St. Catharines.) As a result, Chippawa's period of greatest prosperity was in the 1830s, when a local shipyard manufactured ships and Oliver Macklem's foundry supplied them with engines and boilers. The foundry also made fire engines, milling equipment and stoves. The "Stove Manufactory" was said to be the largest in Upper Canada.

Excitement reached fever pitch in Chippawa in December, 1837, when William Lyon Mackenzie, the rebel leader, set up his provisional government for a Canadian republic on Navy Island, just opposite the village.

Mackenzie was no stranger to the people of the Niagara area. It was in Queenston that he had published the early issues of his famous newspaper the *Colonial Advocate*. He had lived there less than a year, but long enough to cause an amusing scandal. When the foundation for the Brock monument was laid, early in 1824, a glass vessel containing an inscription, and some contemporary newspapers and coins was placed in a hollow under the stone. Mackenzie himself performed the ceremony of depositing the hermetically sealed bottle, placing over it the fur of a beaver. On top of this, the foundation stone was laid, burying the bottle of

80

mementoes for posterity to discover. When Lieutenant-Governor Maitland heard that one of the newspapers enclosed in the bottle was the first number of the *Colonial Advocate* in which he had been castigated by Mackenzie's caustic pen, he was enraged. He ordered the foundation-stone excavated, the bottle opened and the offending newspaper removed, much to editor Mackenzie's amusement. (The handsome stone dwelling, where William Lyon Mackenzie lived and printed his newspaper, has been reconstructed below the heights at Queenston, only a short distance from Laura Secord's house.)

In 1837, the villagers of Chippawa were more alarmed than amused by the sight of Mackenzie's republican tricolour flag with its twin stars representing Upper and Lower Canada, flying in the breeze at Navy Island. They observed the *Caroline* moving back and forth between the island and the American shore, bringing men and supplies. Some of the villagers must have witnessed the subsequent burning of the ship one midnight. All of them heard and felt the reverberations of the bombardment by government forces which finally drove Mackenzie off the island to take refuge in the United States.

Mackenzie's flight did not end the rebel activities. Some of his supporters who lived in the United States and called themselves "Patriots" made raids across the border from time to time. Almost a year after the Navy Island episode, a prominent Chippawa man, Edgeworth Ussher, an outspoken opponent of the rebels, was brutally murdered. Two men, believed to be Patriots, called around two one morning at the Ussher home and shot Edgeworth dead as he opened the door. The following year, raiders again visited Chippawa, and set fire to Trinity Church (now Holy Trinity Church).

These events must have caused consternation at the customs house located on the river front. James Secord, as customs collector, was exposed to danger from the raiders. The provincial authorities feared further acts of violence, and viewed all American aliens with suspicion. James was accused of employing an alien as his deputy collector. He denied the charge in a letter to the Lieutenant-Governor, Sir George Arthur, stating that he had lived more than sixty years in Upper Canada, had been severely wounded, and could call as witness "gentlemen of the first standing in Toronto & elsewhere as to my caracter for Honour, Integrity & Loyalty. . . ." This letter was dated 29 August, 1840.

One would have thought that James Secord's financial responsibilities towards his family would be decreasing by this time, and that his financial situation would consequently improve, but fate conspired against this. His widowed daughters used to come home with their children and live at Chippawa, presumably until they married again. Early in 1840, Mrs. Secord sent a petition to the lieutenant-governor asking for the concession of the ferry at Queenston. "Your Excellency['s] Memorialist," she said, "would not now presume to ask any renumeration [sic], but from the circumstances of having a large family of Daughters & Grand Daughters to provide for & for which the small means of my Husband Captain James Secord Sen'r will not meet. . . ."

Mrs. Secord prefaced her request by narrating the story of her service at Beaver Dams.

That your Excellency's Memorialist did in the Month of June 1813, as the following Certificate of Colonel FitzGibbon will fully coroborate,* did

*Mis-spelled words are as written by Mrs. Secord.

at great Risk peril & danger travelling on foot & partly in the Night by a circuitous route, through woods mountains, the enemys lines & Indian Encampments to give important intelligence of a meditated attack of the Americans upon our troops & by which circumstance has laid the foundation of a desease from which she has never recovered & for which performance your Excellencys Memorialist has never Received the smallest compensation. . . .

Colonel FitzGibbon's certificate, written originally February 23, 1837, said that Mrs. Secord had walked "about 20 miles partly through the Woods" to warn him of the enemy's intended attack "she having obtained such Knowledge from good authority, as the event proved."

Mrs. Secord's petition fell on deaf ears, and she did not get the Queenston ferry.

Suddenly a blow was struck that changed the course of Laura Secord's life. Her husband died on February 22, 1841, in his sixty-eighth year. At his own request, James was buried in Drummond Hill Cemetery, Niagara Falls, scene of the Battle of Lundy's Lane in which his fellow militiamen of Lincoln county had participated.

The Reverend William Leeming of Trinity Church, Chippawa, said of James Secord in his funeral sermon, "he was a conscientious and upright man, amiable in all the relations of life, a kind husband, an indulgent parent, a sincere friend and an obliging neighbour."

8/THE
LONELY
WIDOW

"You can not think what grief we are in," Mrs. Secord wrote to her sister, Mira Hitchcock, a few months after her husband died. Laura was sixty-five, a widow without resources. Her husband's pension as well as his income as customs collector had ceased with his death, and there was no widow's pension.

Laura was so anxious about the future that, a few days after James was buried, she addressed a petition to Governor Sydenham asking that her son Charles be appointed Collector of Customs at Chippawa to succeed her husband. His death, she said, "has left your Memorialist without any means of support and with two daughters and several grand children depending entirely upon her." Charles, now married and living in Queenston, had succeeded his father as Registrar of the Niagara Surrogate Court in 1833. He was not granted the collector's post at Chippawa and his mother sent a second petition to Lord Sydenham asking this time for a pension.

In this lengthy memorial, Laura emphasized her indigence. His Excellency's petitioner, she wrote, "is now far advanced in years and consequently is unable to make much exertion for her own maintenance"; she has been left "totally unprovided for, her dear late husband not having had the means of making a provision for her support"; he had suffered for a long time previous to his death from the effects of his wound "which not only materially injured his shoulder but also his general health." She recounted her own "useful service at the risk of her life" in June 1813, and enclosed the certificate written in 1837 by Colonel James FitzGibbon, testifying to her deed. For this service, she said, she "has never received the slightest remuneration nor has she ever claimed any." (In her previous petitions she had asked for an appointment or a concession but not for money.) She hoped that His Excellency would lay her application before the House of Assembly, and that the Legislature would "view her case favourably and thereby grant her a Pension." The Governor-in-Chief turned down her request, saying that "The Petitioners late Husband enjoyed up to his death a pension of £20* for his wound, besides holding the Situation of Collector of Customs at Chippawa."

How did Mrs. Secord manage to live? We can only hazard a guess. Perhaps she received some income from the land her husband had received as a grant, referred to in the preceding chapter. She may also have inherited land from her father, but what she had she was unable to sell profitably. She said in a letter to her sister Mira three years after her husband's death, that "the lands are mostly sold to the Canada Company. I have given up the idea of trying to do anything about mine." The more prosperous members of Laura's family may have helped her over the most difficult period.

At any rate, towards the end of 1841, Laura bought the house in Chippawa that has been

*Earlier government reports list the pension as £18, as indicated in the previous chapter, p. 73.

associated with her name ever since. It was a charming red brick cottage with a latticed porch, on the corner of Water Street and Adelaide Street (now Laura Secord Place), and fronting on the Chippawa Creek. She bought it for £155 (about $400) from James Cummings, son of Thomas Cummings, Loyalist founder of the village. In this cottage, Mrs. Secord ran a small private school for children. Apparently the school was of brief duration and we may conclude it was not very remunerative.

Laura Secord's house may still be seen in Chippawa, and, though it has undergone alterations over the years, its charm remains. The hand-made orange-red brick has been painted; the cottage roof has been replaced by an end-gable roof with end chimneys. The gables are covered with siding. The latticed rose-covered porch was burned in a fire about 1925 but fortunately the handsome doorway was not spoiled. The glass-panelled door (originally it was solid wood) is flanked by Greek Doric columns and sidelights, and has a rectangular transom. The doorway is now painted cream and on either side of it is a large triple window. There are four large panes of glass in the middle panel of each window replacing the twenty-four small panes in the original sash. A vertical row of six panes in the sidelights flanking the middle panel carries out the original design. Laura's climbing roses over the doorway disappeared with the porch but there is still a climbing rose bush in the spacious yard at the back. Shrubs and trees shade the house.

Only a block away is the central square of the village and Main Street. Within full view of the house is the bridge connecting the east and west halves of the village, and leading to historic Bridgewater Street, at one time part of the Portage Road. If you turn right as you cross the bridge, you come to the Niagara River Parkway, the scenic road to Niagara Falls.

A year after James Secord died, Laura's daughter Harriet lost her husband, and she brought her children to Chippawa to live with her mother. Laura was still lonely and longed to see Mira, who was living in far-off Massachusetts. "My dear Sister," she wrote, "how often I wish I could be near you to tell you my griefs. I feel so lonely; all will soon be in the grave."

Laura was then approaching seventy, a ripe old age in her day. She wore her hair parted in the centre, but like all her contemporaries, she covered it with a bonnet or cap, usually of white cotton and lace-trimmed. Her face with the firm mouth and rather quizzical smile, the straight heavy eyebrows over the dark, sunken eyes, indicated a woman of strong character, one who had experienced much and had drawn her own conclusions. Her grand-daughter, Laura Louisa Smith, described her as "ever sensible and courageous." On one occasion while her husband was customs collector, a party of smugglers was expected to cross the river, and it was feared they might prove dangerous when James seized their goods. Laura put on her husband's over-coat and cap and went to the boat with James and his assistant so that, in the darkness, the smugglers would think there were three men.

Mrs. Secord was noted for her skill in needlework and when her daughters were young, she made their party dresses and long gloves herself, always insisting that their satin slippers match their dresses. "In their prosperous days she was called extravagant," Miss Smith said.

Laura was deeply religious. "If God so decrees" was an expression that frequently recurred in her letters. Her faith helped her to bear the loneliness and privations of her widowhood.

Her service during the War of 1812 was still un-
rewarded and largely unknown, but in 1845 the
first published account of her deed appeared. It
came about in connection with Colonel James Fitz-
Gibbon's efforts to obtain a sum of money as a
reward for *his* services. By this time, FitzGibbon
had advanced in his career. He was a colonel in the
militia; he had served as Assistant Adjutant General
of the Militia in Upper Canada; had been Clerk of
the House of Assembly in Upper Canada for
several years, and was now Clerk of the Legislative
Council of the province of Canada (formerly
Upper and Lower Canada).

The government had discovered that FitzGibbon
had a special flair for dealing with rioters and had
sent him more than once to quell distrubances:
between the Irish and Scottish settlers near Perth,
Ontario; among the immigrants at Peterborough;
during an Orange parade in York; and among the
Irish workers on the Long Sault Canal at Cornwall.
He had a lively confrontation with William Lyon
Mackenzie during a riotous outbreak in York
between two opposing political factions. When Fitz-
Gibbon appeared in the angry crowd, the little
rebel tried to goad him into calling out the troops,
but FitzGibbon refused. Instead he turned to the
crowd and called upon individuals he recognized to
help him maintain order. "I was answered with a
shout of approbation," FitzGibbon said, "and I then
conducted Mr. Mackenzie to his house and shut him
in, having at the door to use force, he endeavouring
to address the multitude which I would not
permit. . . ." What a feat, to silence the irrepressible
William Lyon Mackenzie!

When the rebels, under Mackenzie, marched on
Toronto in December, 1837, it was FitzGibbon
who led the militia in the shattering counter-attack.

The Lieutenant-Governor, Sir Francis Bond Head, had stubbornly refused to admit that the rebels presented any threat to the city, and had even sent all the troops from Upper Canada to the neighbouring province to help put down the rebellion then erupting in Lower Canada. The Governor and his advisers had laughed at FitzGibbon's warnings but turned to him for help, nevertheless, when the crisis came. Chief Justice John Beverley Robinson, a stalwart member of the Family Compact, said afterwards that "I have no doubt . . . that his [Fitz-Gibbon's] earnest conviction before the outbreak, that violence would be attempted, and the measures of precaution which he spontaneously took in consequence of that impression were the means of saving the Government and the loyal Inhabitants of Toronto from being, for a time at least at the mercy of the Rebels. . . ."

As a result of this dramatic event the government decided at last to reward Colonel FitzGibbon for his "signal services to this Province in a Military capacity." The legislature passed a bill granting him five thousand acres of land, but the Queen refused to give assent to the bill on technical grounds. In 1845 the government proposed to set the matter straight by awarding FitzGibbon a thousand pounds in lieu of the land grant. When the bill came up for discussion in the House of Assembly, it did not have clear sailing, though it passed finally with a large majority. One member objected on the ground that, at Beaver Dams, FitzGibbon "had monopolized honor which did not rightfully belong to him." This annoyed Laura Secord's son, Charles, and he wrote the letter to *The Church* in April, 1845, which was mentioned in a previous chapter.* Charles Secord told how his mother, after hearing

*See p. 49.

the American officers talking of their plan to capture FitzGibbon, walked on foot all the way to Beaver Dams to warn him. "Col. FitzGibbon in consequence of this information prepared himself to meet the enemy," Secord stated, "and soon after the attack being made the American troops were captured and one or two field-pieces taken. . . ." As proof that he was telling the truth, Secord enclosed a certificate written for his mother by Colonel James FitzGibbon in February, 1837. A brief extract from this certificate has already been quoted* but here is the complete text.

> I do hereby certify that Mrs. Secord, wife of James Secord of Chippawa, Esquire, did in the month of June, 1813, walk from her house in the village of St. Davids to DeCoo's house in Thorold, by a circuitous route of about twenty miles, partly through the woods, to acquaint me that the enemy intended to attempt by surprise to capture a detachment of the 49th Regiment, then under my command, she having obtained such knowledge from good authority, as the event proved. Mrs. Secord was a person of slight and delicate frame and made this effort in weather excessively warm, and I dreaded at the time that she must suffer in health in consequence of fatigue and anxiety, she having been exposed to danger from the enemy, through whose line of communication she had to pass. The attempt was made on my detachment by the enemy, and his detachment, consisting of upwards of 500 men, with a field piece and 50 dragoons were captured in consequence. I write this certificate in a moment of much hurry and from memory, and it is therefore thus brief.

---

*See p. 58

It will be noted that FitzGibbon was under the impression that Laura Secord lived at St. David's. In the excitement of her arrival she had probably told him she had walked from St. David's, referring to the second and major part of her journey.

The public apparently paid little attention to Charles Secord's letter and his mother continued living in obscurity. Eight years later, however, the story of Laura's walk appeared in another periodical, and this time it was written by no less a person than Laura herself. It was in connection with a "History of the War of 1812" that was running as a serial in the *Anglo-American Magazine**. The author, Gilbert Auchinleck, explained in a footnote that "The circumstances connected with the affair at the Beaver Dam, where Col. Fitzgibbon (then Lieut. Fitzgibbon) gained so much praise for the victory achieved by him over the Americans, was owing to information which Mrs. Secord, the widow of James Secord, Esq., deceased, formerly of Queenston, who was wounded at the battle of that place . . . obtained from private sources of the intention of the American troops to surround and take Fitzgibbon and party. . . ." Following this note was the account which the author had obtained from Laura Secord, along with FitzGibbon's certificate. Parts of Laura's account appeared in Chapter 5, but it is of sufficient interest to be given here in full.

I shall commence at the battle of Queenston, where I was at the time the cannon balls were flying around me in every direction. I left the place during the engagement. After the battle I returned to Queenston, and then found that my husband had been wounded; my house plundered

*November 1853, pp. 466-7; published as a book under the title *The War of 1812* (Toronto, Chewett, 1862).

and property destroyed. It was while the Americans had possession of the frontier, that I learned the plans of the American commander, and determined to put the British troops under Fitzgibbon in possession of them, and if possible, to save the British troops from capture, or, perhaps, total destruction. In doing so I found I should have great difficulty in getting through the American guards, which were out ten miles in the country. Determined to persevere, however, I left early in the morning, walked nineteen miles in the month of June, over a rough and difficult part of the country, when I came to a field belonging to a Mr. Decamp [DeCew], in the neighbourhood of the Beaver Dam. By this time daylight had left me. Here I found all the Indians encamped; by moonlight the scene was terrifying, and to those accustomed to such scenes, might be considered grand. Upon advancing to the Indians they all rose, and, with some yells, said "Woman," which made me tremble. I cannot express the awful feeling it gave me; but I did not lose my presence of mind. I was determined to persevere. I went up to one of the chiefs, made him understand that I had great news for Capt. Fitzgibbon, and that he must let me pass to his camp, or that he and his party would be all taken. The chief at first objected to let me pass, but finally consented, after some hesitation, to go with me and accompany me to Fitzgibbon's station, which was at the Beaver Dam, where I had an interview with him. I then told him what I had come for, and what I had heard — that the Americans intended to make an attack upon the troops under his command, and would, from their superior numbers, capture them all. Benefitting by this information Capt. Fitzgibbon formed his plans accordingly, and captured about five hundred American infantry, about fifty mounted dragoons, and a field-piece or two was taken from the enemy. I returned home next day, exhausted and fatigued. I am now advanced in years, and when I look back I wonder how I could have gone through so much fatigue, with the fortitude to accomplish it.

Laura's deed had now been drawn to the attention of the public for the second time but it would be a mistake to think that her name immediately became a household word. Far from it. One history textbook picked up the story and made a brief reference to Mrs. Secord's walk in connection with the Battle of Beaver Dams, but it was in parenthesis as if unimportant. It stated simply that Mrs. Secord had "walked 13 miles to apprise the British officer of the expedition sent against him."* Recognition for Laura Secord was on the way, however. The climax of her long life was still to come.

*J. George Hodgins, *The Geography and History of British America and of the Other Colonies of the Empire* (Toronto, Maclear, 1857), p. 61.

9/THE
PRINCE COMES
TO THE RESCUE

On a September evening in 1860, Laura Secord, now a little old lady of eighty-five, put on a black silk dress and her best muslin bonnet, threw a shawl over her shoulders, and stepped out onto the porch of her cottage, accompanied by her fifty-eight-year-old daughter Charlotte. After locking the door (for there were many strangers in the village that evening), the two women went briskly down the front path, their full tent-like skirts swaying as they walked and barely clearing the ground. Charlotte took her mother's arm protectively, as they crossed the wooden bridge, though she herself was showing signs of age, and her mother was still quite alert and capable of getting about by herself. They remarked on the size of the crowd that had already gathered on the other side of Chippawa Creek.

When they reached the west side, the two women turned right, making their way in the twilight towards Macklem's wharf where the Prince of Wales' ship was to dock. It was not expected for another hour at least but the air was full of excitement. For weeks the people of the Niagara area had been looking forward to the thrilling moment when His Royal Highness, Albert Edward, Prince of Wales, eldest son of Queen Victoria, would step onto their soil. The villagers of Chippawa were elated that the prince had chosen to land first at their port rather than at Queenston or Niagara.

He had been touring British North America for over a month, beginning at St. John's, Newfoundland in July, and gradually coming west by ship and train, visiting Halifax, Quebec, Montreal, Ottawa, Toronto and points in between. On this particular day, Friday, September 14, the Royal train had taken the prince through the beautiful fall countryside of Western Ontario to London, Ingersoll, Woodstock, Paris, Brantford and finally, Fort Erie. There he was to transfer to the steamer *Clifton* for the short voyage down the Niagara River to Chippawa.

A red carpet had been spread on Macklem's wharf for the Royal feet to step on. A rope prevented the crowd from getting too close to the red carpet and the reception area, but the Secord women worked their way as close to the dock as possible. They could see the familiar figure of their neighbour, James Cummings, Warden of Welland county, standing in the midst of the official welcoming party — the councillors and magistrates of Lincoln and Welland counties.

When it began to get dark on the wharf, some people lit torches which they held high in their hands. The flickering flames cast a gay light over the scene, and at the same time added a touch of mystery. Mrs. Secord and Charlotte were both short, and it seemed to them that everyone was pushing against them or deliberately moving in front of them to obscure their view. Suddenly there was a commotion as a group of firemen rushed to the dock with large flaming torches to illuminate the landing place. The *Clifton* had been sighted moving slowly down the Niagara River. As it

95

turned into Chippawa Creek, everyone stood on tiptoe, necks craned, to catch a glimpse of the ship and, if possible, of the nineteen-year-old prince, the future King Edward VII.

When the slender young man in plain clothes finally stepped onto the wharf, three welcoming cheers rang out. The prince "courteously acknowledged them by raising his hat and glanced round with that pleasant good-natured look of his that has won all hearts for him in Upper Canada," the *Niagara Mail* reported. Prince Edward made his way with the official party towards the carriage that was to take him to the reception at the Pavilion Hotel, while men doffed their hats and ladies waved their white handkerchiefs. Everyone sang "God Save the Queen."

A gay procession of lighted carriages and torch-bearing pedestrians started moving towards the Pavilion Hotel on the Drummondville common (where the Seagram Tower of Niagara Falls now stands). Laura and Charlotte were not among them. They sauntered slowly back along the river bank and over the bridge to their cottage, thrilled with their first sight of the handsome young prince, and anticipating the opportunities they would have in the next few days to see him again, perhaps even to meet him.

Meanwhile the procession arrived at the hotel where an open pavilion had been set up for the official reception. After the address of welcome and the prince's brief response, a few people were presented to him and then the carriages proceeded through the decorated streets to the residence of the late Samuel Zimmerman, the wealthy railway contractor. His house stood on a buff high above the falls in what is now Queen Victoria Park. It had been specially decorated and furnished for the

96

prince's use during his stay at Niagara Falls. From the verandah of the house, His Royal Highness could view the turbulent waters of the Niagara as they tumbled over the giant horseshoe.

In honour of the prince, the falls were illuminated that night, probably for the first time in history. Bengal fires and blue lights created a truly magical effect and the people were ecstatic over the sight. The *Niagara Mail* said,

> The American and Canadian Falls, Goat Island with its thick woods and the deep chasm of the river and the foaming rapids above suddenly emerged from the surrounding darkness and presented a spectacle which can never be forgotten by those who witnessed it. The Prince stood on the verandah of his house enraptured with the sight than which the world could not offer one more grand. This was his first view of the Falls and will never be forgotten by him.

Nor was the prince likely to forget the spectacle he saw the next day — the daring stunt of Blondin, the French tightrope walker, crossing above the rapids on a rope, not once but twice. First he carried a man on his back, and then he crossed on stilts. Everyone held his breath when Blondin slipped, while on stilts, and nearly fell. But he caught his thigh on the rope, regained his position, and completed the crossing. "Some said this was done for effect," the Toronto *Globe* reported, "but if so, the manoeuvre was admirably executed, inasmuch that many ladies actually averted their eyes that they might not see the man fall into the rapids."

On Sunday the prince drove in his carriage to Chippawa to attend service at Holy Trinity Church. This was the church that the "Patriots" had burned in 1839 but the congregation had rebuilt it two years later. Laura Secord was a regular worshipper in the church and we may be sure that the devout old lady was in her pew that Sunday morning to worship with the prince. The clergyman who had conducted her husband's funeral service, the Reverend William Leeming, preached the sermon.

Was Mrs. Secord presented to Prince Edward after the morning service? Did he call on her at her cottage? Reports are conflicting, but it is certain that she hoped to be presented to the prince some time during his stay at Niagara Falls. She prepared a memorial for the occasion, which was filed with the Governor General before the prince's arrival, as was required.

Laura began her memorial by saying, "Having the privilege accorded me this day of presenting myself before your Royal Highness I beg to assure you that I do so with the greatest gratification to my feelings. I am confident your Royal Highness will pardon the liberty I have taken when your Royal Highness is informed of the circumstances which have led me to do so." Then she described the service she had performed for the British in the War of 1812, and continued:

I am now a very old woman — a widow many years. A few short years even if I should so long live will see me no more upon this earth. I feel that it will be gratifying to my family and a pleasure to myself that your Royal Parent the Queen should know that the services which I performed were truly loyal and that no gain or hope of reward influenced me in doing what I did.

I request that your Royal Highness will be pleased to convey to your Royal Parent Her Majesty the Queen the name of one who in the hour of trial and danger — as well as my departed husband who fought and bled on Queenston Heights in the ever memorable battle of 13th Oct. 1812 — stood ever ready and willing to defend this Country against every invasion come what might.

The memorial closed with polite good wishes for the prince and his "Royal Parent." Attached was the 1837 certificate by James FitzGibbon and appended to it was this statement by Warden James Cummings:

I Certify that I have for many years, been personally acquainted with Mrs. Secord named in the above Certificate; and that she is the person she represents herself to be in her Memorial hereunto annexed. And further she is a person of the most Respectable Character. — Chippawa 10th Septem'r 1860.

Whether or not Mrs. Secord handed her memorial to the prince in person, is not known, but her name was drawn to his attention in another way as well. It was on the address presented by the veterans of the War of 1812 at Queenston Heights on September 18. This ceremony was the biggest event of the Prince of Wales' visit to the Niagara area. Militia veterans assembled from all parts of the province for the occasion. In the morning, over 500 visitors including veterans, came to Queenston on the steamer *Peerless* from Toronto and Port Dalhousie. On docking at Queenston about 10:00 *a.m.*, the militia companies "formed into a procession, and headed by a band of music, commenced their march up the steep, narrow, winding road to the Heights. As the heat was now very strong, this was by no means a task of pleasure," said the *Mail*. "The grounds around the monument was [*sic*] thronged. . . . Hundreds of waggons were laid up in ordinary under the shade of the trees, while their owners were ranged in thick masses along each side of the road by which the Prince was expected to arrive." The platform, which had been erected on the south side of Brock's monument, was flanked by rifle companies. Just below the platform in the place of honour, stood the militia veterans of the War of 1812 "all old men, dressed for the most part in a blue uniform, with steel epaulettes and glazed caps." Some were in plain clothes.

The prince arrived in his Royal carriage shortly after 11 o'clock, but so great was the crush of the eager and cheering crowd that the carriage could not proceed, and he and his entourage were forced to get out and walk to their places on the platform. Chief Justice Sir John Beverley Robinson, a distinguished militia veteran, read the address and after the prince had responded "with mingled feelings of pride and pain" (his words), the Chief Justice escorted him inside the monument where he climbed the 185 steps to the top "to enjoy one of the most magnificent sights that any country can produce" (*Niagara Mail*).

An important ceremony was still to come. At the foot of the Heights, the prince laid a large stone to commemorate the spot where Sir Isaac Brock fell on October 13, 1812. This stone, on a solid square base, surrounded by an iron chain held in place by four small iron posts, stands in Queenston on Clarence Street, just north of No. 8A Highway, and only a short distance from the Secord house.

It is not known whether Laura Secord went to Queenston for the ceremony at the Heights, but she had made sure that her name was among those of the veterans attached to the address. She had gone to the office of the Clerk of the Peace at Niagara a month previously to sign her name. The *Niagara Mail* described what had happened: "The Clerk demurred to taking so novel a signature, although the lady insisted on her right, having done her country more signal service during the war than half the soldiers and militiamen engaged in it." The determined little woman had her way and it was said that this sole female signature on the address was drawn to the attention of the prince and aroused his interest in Laura Secord. Perhaps he had already read her memorial. He may even have met her.

The prince did not forget Mrs. Secord when he returned to England. As the *Mail* put it, "The Prince of Wales is a true, gallant Prince, with a warm regard for the old ladies as well as for the young ones." Early in 1861, he sent Laura a gift of one hundred pounds in gold, and this was the only financial reward Laura Secord ever received for her heroic deed. She had waited nearly fifty years for it.

10/LAURA BECOMES FAMOUS

If the year had been 1961 instead of 1861, Laura Secord would have become famous overnight. Her face, lined with life's wrinkles, and encircled by the white lace of her bonnet, would have shone forth from the television screen in everyone's home. Her voice would have been heard responding to questions about her walk to Beaver Dams. Every newspaper in the country would have published the story of the Prince of Wales' gift, copiously illustrated with pictures of the youthful prince and the grandmotherly heroine.

As it was, fame came slowly. The *Niagara Mail* covered the story in one paragraph. Describing Laura as "the widow of the late Jas. Secord, Esq., of Chippawa," it said, "Her patriotic services during the War of 1812, which are well known, [and] were brought under the notice of the Prince during his visit last summer, have thus been handsomely acknowledged." The following week, the *Mail* admitted that not everyone knew what Mrs. Secord had done: "A correspondent wants to know what particular services were rendered by Mrs. Secord of Chippawa . . . which have led to the handsome present of £100 from the Prince of Wales. . . ." The paper then reprinted an account from the *Welland Reporter* which said, in part:

During the war of 1812-13, Mrs. Secord who was quite a young woman at the time, was living on a farm about mid-way between Queenston and St. Davids, both of which places were at that period occupied by American troops. During their frequent visits at their house she overheard them planning a surprise and night attack upon a detachment of British soldiers stationed near the Beaverdams, under the command of Lieut. Fitzgibbon. Without betraying any knowledge of the affair, this brave woman set off by night through the woods, a distance of thirteen miles to the British camp notwithstanding the imminent peril of falling into the hands of the American scouts or hostile Indians, and gave the British commander such information as enabled him to successfully repel the attack and defeat the Americans with great slaughter. . . . Mrs. S. is now over eighty years of age, in possession of all her faculties, and she yet takes much pleasure in recounting her adventures upon the occasion above alluded to. The gift of the Prince will doubtless afford much satisfaction, as well to the members of her family and other relatives as to her many friends by whom she is held in much esteem. We trust the old lady may long be spared to the unimpaired enjoyment of all the comforts of this life.

This account was not quite accurate (Mrs. Secord, by her own testimony, was living in Queenston in June 1813, and she did not "set off by night"), but it gave the main facts. From now on, the name of Laura Secord appeared in print with increasing frequency. The historian, Gilbert Auchinleck, as has been noted, had already published her own narrative, but it was the prince who provided the magic touch that transformed "the widow of the

103

late James Secord" into the heroine, Laura Secord. After the transformation came the legend and the confusion of fact with fancy.

Since Laura Secord's walk was to become the subject of controversy in later years, it is interesting to observe the variety of ways in which stories of her deed reached the public and how they contributed to the legend.

Three years after Mrs. Secord received her royal gift, the first book to treat her as a heroine made its appearance. The author was William F. Coffin, and his book was the one previously mentioned, *1812: the War and its Moral*. As we have seen, Coffin took an imaginative view of history and added trimmings to the Laura Secord episode to make it more exciting. Perhaps it was because Coffin was a highly placed government official (he was commissioner of Ordinance Lands for Canada and a lieutenant-colonel in the militia), that people were so ready to believe he told the facts. Actually, his account was a *mélange* of real and imaginative happenings. His most obvious mistake was to call Mrs. Secord "Mary."

According to Coffin, it was James who heard of the American plan to attack FitzGibbon, and he "hobbled home to his wife with the news." Husband and wife agreed that FitzGibbon must be warned. James could not go, but his wife "Mrs. Mary Secord" spoke out saying she would go herself.

At three in the morning she was up, got ready the children's breakfast, and taking a cracker and cup of coffee, started after day break. To have left earlier would have aroused suspicion. Her first difficulty was the American advanced sentry. He was hard to deal with, but she pointed to her own farm buildings a little in advance of his post, insisted that she was going for milk; told him he could watch her, and was allowed to pass on. She did milk a cow, which was very *contrary*, and would persist in moving onwards to the edge of the opposite bushes, into which both she and the cow disappeared. Once out of sight, she pushed on rapidly.

Coffin went on to describe Mrs. Secord's walk through the woods, her fear of wolves and rattlesnakes, how she crossed a brook on a log, how she called on a miller's wife who tried to dissuade her from continuing, how she encountered a British sentry and finally the Indians. The author gave the impression that he had heard the details from the heroine herself. "Mrs. Mary Secord . . . at the age of 88, still lives in the village of Chippawa, to tell the story, and wakes up into young life as she does so," he said. Compare this with the statement already quoted from the *Welland Reporter:* "Mrs. S. is now over eighty years of age, in possession of all her faculties, and she yet takes much pleasure in recounting her adventures." Note also that the farm appears in both accounts. We may surmise that Coffin borrowed at least some of his "facts" from the *Reporter* article.

In any event, people liked Coffin's version of the story. The cow fitted the pioneer picture perfectly, and it was only a matter of time until it became an inseparable part of the Laura Secord legend. Few people today have ever heard of William F. Coffin or his book, but mention Laura Secord and they think immediately of the woman with the cow.

Laura was now well on the way to fame. She had achieved recognition and a monetary reward; she had begun to wear the halo of a heroine; but she was not permitted to live to enjoy the full glory of celebrity. Laura Secord died on October 17, 1868.

Her obituary in the *Niagara Mail* was brief.

DIED

At Chippewa on the 17th Oct. inst. aged 91 years [actually 93] — Mrs. Secord, relict of the late James Secord Esq. Mrs. Secord was one of the Canadian women of the war of 1812, whose spirit and devotion to their country contributed so much to its defence. Having ascertained during the night that a large American force under Colonel Boerstler was proceeding in the direction of the Beaver dams, in the Niagara district, Mrs. Secord hastened on foot through the dense forest, and in the night — a distance of twenty miles — to inform Colonel FitzGibbon — then in command of a small force of British troops and Indians — of the movement of the enemy. Acting on this information, Colonel FitzGibbon marched at once to intercept the enemy, and at daylight next morning encountered, defeated and captured the whole force under Colonel Boerstler, in the battle known as that of the Beech Woods. At the visit of the Prince of Wales to Canada in 1860, Mrs. Secord was introduced to him, and received from him a substantial token of his respect for her patriotism and intrepidity.

Mrs. Secord was buried beside her husband in Drummond Hill Cemetery, Lundy's Lane, Niagara Falls.

It will be observed that even the obituary contributed to the false notions that were to add fuel to the future controversy. Mrs. Secord "hastened on foot through the dense forest, and in the night," the obituary said — surely an impossible feat even for the bravest woman, and one that Laura never claimed for herself.

A year after Laura Secord's death, a straightforward account of the part she played in the victory at Beaver Dams appeared in Benson J. Lossing's *Pictorial Field-Book of the War of 1812.** The book had been in preparation for several years, and, in this sense, pre-dated Coffin's history.

Lossing was an American historian and artist who visited Canada in the 1860s accumulating first-hand information for his history. He travelled through the Niagara Peninsula visiting battle scenes, interviewing veterans and other residents, and making sketches of battle sites. He asked Mrs. Secord for a personal account of her walk and for a photograph of herself. She complied with both. She sent him a daguerrotype which was delivered to him by J. P. Merritt, son of W. Hamilton Merritt whose sister, it will be recalled, had married Laura's brother, Charles Ingersoll. This picture is one of two authentic portraits of Laura Secord in existence today. It had obviously been taken some years before the publication of Lossing's book as it shows a much younger Mrs. Secord than one past ninety.

The narrative Laura Secord sent to Lossing was similar to the one she had prepared in 1853 for Auchinleck but it showed signs of her advancing years and weakening memory. It was dated February 18, 1861, and it was probably written for her by her granddaughter, Laura Louisa Smith, who based it on the 1853 letter. There was one notable difference between the two accounts. Whereas in the earlier letter, Mrs. Secord had said, "I found I *should have* great difficulty in getting through the

*New York, Harper, 1869.

American guards," in 1861 she said, "I *had* much difficulty in getting through the American Guards."* Did the granddaughter make this change in the wording to emphasize her grandmother's heroism, not realizing, of course, the historic significance of what she was doing?

A copy of Mrs. Secord's 1861 letter is in the Public Archives of Canada. It is longer than the edited version that Lossing published, and it is prefaced by this paragraph written in the third person: "Mr. Lossing will find in the Anglo American Magazine a certificate given by Colonel Fitzgibbon to Mrs. Secord, to show what she had done towards saving her country, but as Mr. Lossing wishes a relation given by herself, she has much pleasure in doing so, as far as her memory will allow, which she thanks God she still retains." A postscript in similar vein was added, also in the third person: "Mrs. Secord trusts Mr. Lossing will find what she has stated to his satisfaction; there are many other little incidents during the last American War, might be told, but thinks it useless at present."

There is no indication who wrote these two paragraphs but it was undoubtedly the same hand that wrote the main part of the letter in the first person.

Like Auchinleck, Lossing placed Mrs. Secord's account at the bottom of the page in a footnote, along with FitzGibbon's certificate, but he drew attention to her account by describing her deed in his own words in the main body of the text. On the same page, Mrs. Secord's picture brought the impact of reality.

Later historians of the War of 1812 and writers of school histories, gave credit to Laura Secord for the victory at Beaver Dams. Usually the cow

*Italics added.

108

appeared in the narrative. Even so painstaking a historian as Colonel E. A. Cruikshank accepted the cow as authentic and, for good measure, added the milkpail. In his *Fight in the Beechwoods*, a detailed account of the Battle of Beaver Dams, Cruikshank said, "Leaving the house at the first flush of dawn, with a pail upon her arm, she [Laura Secord] succeeded in passing the nearest sentinel under pretence of milking a cow in the fields beyond. It was then no difficult matter to guide the animal behind a convenient thicket, and once fairly out of sight, she threw the pail aside and began her toilsome walk."*

Laura Secord had found her niche in Canadian history as the agent of victory at Beaver Dams. It was a distinctive niche because it was held by a woman, and in the next two decades women played a large part in bringing the name of Laura Secord into prominence as a great Canadian heroine.

Among the women, two writers stand out: Mrs. Sarah Anne Curzon and Mrs. Emma A. Currie. Mrs. Curzon was a versatile writer of English birth who lived in Toronto. She was noted as a fighter for women's rights. In addition to advocating the franchise, she urged that women be admitted to university, whether in arts, science or medicine. Her first work on Laura Secord was a drama in blank verse: *Laura Secord, the Heroine of 1812*, published in 1887. It was neither great poetry nor great drama, but it attracted attention to Laura Secord's heroic deed, and for the first time, Mrs. Secord was presented in a family setting. Husband and children were portrayed on the stage. Succes-

---

*Lundy's Lane Historical Society, 1889, p. 15. Twelve years later, however, in reviewing Mrs. Currie's biography of Laura Secord, Cruikshank expressed some skepticism saying "Tradition . . . should be accepted with great caution."

sive scenes showed American soldiers calling at the Second home demanding a meal; Laura starting out on her journey and encountering an American sentry ("But surely I may go to milk my cow,/Yonder she is . . . ."); her visit at St. David's; her walk through the woods; her encounter with the Indians; and her meeting with FitzGibbon, upon which she faints dramatically. FitzGibbon speaks the closing words after the victory is won at Beaver Dams "thanks to a brave woman's glorious deed."

Mrs. Curzon extolled Laura Secord again in a lengthy poem of rhyming four-line verses, entitled "A Ballad of 1812." Other poets of the day also praised Laura. Two of the best known were the patriotic poets Agnes Maule Machar of Kingston, Ontario and Charles Mair, author of the poetic drama "Tecumseh." Miss Machar's poem "Laura Secord" depicted the heroine as a warm, motherly woman, "bending o'er her babes" and "smiling through her tears," but above all, courageous. "These are not times for brave men's wives/To yield to craven fears," she said, as she resolved to take the message to FitzGibbon. Charles Mair paid his tribute to Laura Secord in "A Ballad for Brave Women." The sentiment of this poem was more noble than the verse which, with its insistent rhyme, jingled more than it sang. It ended on an inspirational note:

> *When her sons lift the linstock and brandish the sword*
> *Her daughters will think of brave Laura Secord.*

As for Mrs. Curzon, her most lasting contribution to the literature on Laura Secord, proved to be a short biography in prose, called *The Story of Laura Secord, 1813* which was published under the auspices of the Lundy's Lane Historical Society in 1891. The author gave information on Laura's background and the Ingersoll family, but she offered little on Mrs. Secord's life at Queenston or Chippawa. In describing the heroine's walk to Beaver Dams, Mrs. Curzon resorted to the sort of melodrama that coloured her poetic play. We see Laura "leaving her home, her sick husband and young children — not without many a scalding tear"; on her way she "traversed the haunted depths of an impenetrable swamp, alone, hungry, faint, and, for the most part of the way, ragged and shoeless." After crossing Twelve Mile Creek on a fallen tree and emerging into a clearing, suddenly she is "surrounded by ambushed Indians, and the chief throws up his tomahawk to strike"; but "at length she reaches FitzGibbon, delivers and verifies her message, and faints."

Mrs. Curzon quoted testimonials from women who knew or had written about Mrs. Secord. Of greatest interest was a statement by Mrs. Harriet Smith, Laura's third daughter. Part of this has been quoted earlier but owing to its special interest, the whole extract is given here:

> I remember seeing my mother leave the house on that fateful morning, but neither I nor my sisters knew exactly on what errand she was bent. She had on house slippers and a flowered print gown; I think it was brown, with orange flowers; at least a yellow tint is connected in my mind with that particular morning.

When Mrs. Curzon wrote the biography, she had a serious purpose in view. She explained, "We have approached our Provincial Legislature for a grant to be expended on marking her [Mrs. Secord's] last resting-place, in Drummondville Cemetery, with a

111

memorial stone somewhat worthy of her and of us. We are ready to open a subscription list. . . ."

It was ten years before the monument was erected and in 1900 a second, more important biography, was published. This was *The Story of Laura Secord, and Canadian Reminiscences*, by Emma A. Currie. The author, born Emma Harvey, was a native of Niagara. She had gone to school in St. David's, and was well acquainted with the history of the Niagara Peninsula. Mrs. Currie was the founder of the Women's Literary Club of St. Catharines. She was active in church and charitable organizations, and, like Mrs. Curzon, was an advocate of woman suffrage.

Mrs. Currie's book is still the standard biography of Laura Secord. The author took great pains to assemble facts about the Ingersoll and Secord families and about Laura's own life. She dealt with Laura's walk objectively, avoiding emotional overtones. Among the people whom Mrs. Currie interviewed while collecting her material was Laura Secord's great-niece, Mrs. Elizabeth Ann Gregory, whose denial of the cow has already been quoted.* A granddaughter of Laura's, Mrs. Isaac Cockburn, gave a personal description: "Laura Secord was of fair complexion, with kind, brown eyes [said by Laura's daughter Harriet, on another occasion, to be dark blue], a sweet and loving smile hovering about the mouth. This did not denote weakness. She was five feet four inches tall and slight in form."

A portrait of Mrs. Secord as an old lady formed the frontispiece of Mrs. Currie's book. The sober, rather sad face, is encircled by a white muslin bonnet decorated with rows of fine ruching and tied under the chin with an ample bow. Her hair, still dark, is parted in the middle. The author com-

See p. 54.

mented on the portrait in her "Introduction," saying it was from "a plate furnished by Rev. Canon Bull, Niagara Falls South. The late Mr. Joel Lyons, of Chippewa, had a likeness of Mrs. Secord, taken in what year is not known, and from this the plate was made." A copy of this portrait may be seen in the historical museum at Niagara-on-the-Lake.*

Mrs. Currie donated all the proceeds of her book to the erection of the monument at Queenston Heights. This was the second monument to Laura Secord. The first was unveiled in Drummond Hill Cemetery, Lundy's Lane, on June 22, 1901.

Thousands of individuals — men, women and children — contributed to the Lundy's Lane monument. Even before Mrs. Curzon had broached the subject, the Stamford High School had begun the memorial fund. The Lundy's Lane and Ontario Historical Societies took it up and solicited contributions from school children, women's groups and others. Nearly a thousand dollars were collected in sums ranging from a dime to fifty dollars. A competition was held for the design of the monument. The award went to the painter and sculptor, Mildred Peel, sister of the well-known Canadian painter Paul Peel. Miss Peel executed a bronze bust of Laura as a young woman, which was placed on an upright granite pedestal. The 8-foot-high monument stands in Drummond Hill Cemetery near the imposing 40-foot granite shaft of the soldiers' monument commemorating those who died in the Battle of Lundy's Lane. This is the inscription on the Laura Secord monument:

TO PERPETUATE / THE NAME AND FAME OF / LAURA SECORD / WHO WALKED ALONE NEARLY

---

*A different and less authentic portrait appeared in the 1913 edition of Mrs. Currie's book.

20 / MILES BY A CIRCUITOUS, DIFFICULT / AND
PERILOUS ROUTE THROUGH WOODS / AND SWAMPS
AND OVER MIRY ROADS / TO WARN A BRITISH OUT-
POST AT / DE CEW'S FALLS OF AN INTENDED AT-
TACK/AND THEREBY ENABLED LIEUT. FITZGIBBON
/ON THE 24TH JUNE, 1813, WITH LESS/THAN 50
MEN OF H.M. 49TH REGT. / ABOUT 15 MILITIA-
MEN AND A SMALL / FORCE OF SIX NATION AND
OTHER INDIANS/UNDER CAPTAINS WILLIAM JOHN-
SON KERR / AND DOMINIQUE DUCHARME, TO SUR-
PRISE/AND ATTACK THE ENEMY AT BEECHWOODS/
(OR BEAVER DAMS), AND AFTER A SHORT/ENGAGE-
MENT TO CAPTURE COL. BOERSTLER / OF THE
U.S. ARMY AND HIS ENTIRE FORCE / OF 542 MEN
WITH TWO FIELD PIECES.

The monument replaced the two small marble
slabs that had marked the graves of Mr. and Mrs.
Secord. The inscriptions on the slabs bearing the
names, birth and death dates of James and Laura
were copied on two sides of the monument, and the
slabs were transferred to Holy Trinity Church,
Chippawa, where they may be seen today.

The second Laura Secord monument, to which
reference has been made, was erected on Queenston
Heights in 1910, by the Government of Canada.
This 12-foot-high gray granite memorial is more
imposing than the one at Lundy's Lane. It stands on
the cliff a short distance from the soaring Brock
column, and is set apart in a small square attrac-
tively bordered with a low hedge and surrounded
by shrubs and flower beds. A bronze medallion on
the front of the monument depicts the head and
shoulders of the elderly, bonneted Mrs. Secord. The
simple inscription reads:

TO LAURA INGERSOLL SECORD / WHO SAVED HER
HUSBAND'S LIFE / IN THE BATTLE OF THESE
HEIGHTS / OCTOBER 13TH, 1812/AND WHO RISK-

114

ED HER OWN / IN CONVEYING TO CAPT. FITZ-
GIBBON/INFORMATION BY WHICH HE WON/THE
VICTORY OF BEAVER DAMS.

In its description of the unveiling ceremony, on July 5, 1911, the Toronto *Globe* said, "Three thousand Canadians, in the presence of not a few United States visitors from Buffalo, Lewiston, and other centres, to-day honored perhaps their greatest heroine, Laura Secord, to whose memory the Dominion Government has erected a monument on a superb site at Queenston Heights." Several descendants of Mrs. Secord's attended the ceremony, and among the other noted guests were her biographer Mrs. J. G. Currie (Mrs. Curzon was no longer living), and a future Governor-General, Lieutenant Vincent Massey.

Laura Secord's name and fame had gone a long way since those days eighty years ago when her greatest ambition had been to be assigned the care of Brock's monument! Little had she dreamed that the government of a greater Canada than the one that had spurned her, would erect a monument in her honour, or that her sculptured face would share the glory of Queenston Heights with the hero she revered — Sir Isaac Brock.

The Ontario Government also paid tribute to the heroine. It did her the unprecedented honour (for a woman) of having her portrait painted and hung in the Parliament Building at Toronto. Mildred Peel was commissioned to do the painting in 1905. She portrayed Mrs. Secord as an elderly woman, a bonnet on her head, lace mitts on her hands. According to a contemporary account in the *Christian Guardian*, "Miss Peel, availing herself of existing likenesses, also made a careful study of the faces of a number of living relatives, and has succeeded in producing a portrait as faithful to the original as

115

could now be had. . . ." The colours of the portrait were dark and subdued, and, except for the bonnet and lace mitts, the picture bore little resemblance to the photographs of Mrs. Secord that are known to be authentic.

Nevertheless it was a great honour for Laura Secord to be singled out by the Ontario Government to have her portrait hung in the hall of fame between those of Sir Isaac Brock and the Honourable George Brown, a Father of Confederation. One newspaper commented, "It has taken years of persevering effort, inaugurated by Mrs. Curzon and carried on by the women of Ontario, to place Laura Ingersoll Secord in the Parliament Buildings of Ontario."

Mrs. Currie gave the credit to the Premier. In the "Introduction" to the revised edition of her book, she said, "Sir George Ross deserves the gratitude of Canadian women for placing in the Parliament Buildings of Ontario the portrait of Laura Ingersoll Secord, and procuring the grant from the Dominion Government which made the Memorial on Queenston Heights possible."

The portrait was destined to stir up an amusing controversy two decades later, as we shall see in the next chapter. In the meantime it is of interest to note that in 1907, Mildred Peel became Sir George Ross's third wife.

It is not possible to give the names of all the women who helped to bring Laura Secord to the peak of her fame but three more should be mentioned — Mary Agnes FitzGibbon, Mrs. E. J. Thompson and Miss Janet Carnochan.

The first of these was the author of *A Veteran of 1812, the Life of James FitzGibbon.** The famous soldier was her grandfather. On her mother's side,

*Toronto, Briggs, 1894.

116

Mary Agnes FitzGibbon had an equally famous grandmother, Mrs. Susanna Moodie, author of the Canadian classic, *Roughing It in the Bush*. It might be expected that Miss FitzGibbon would have some inside information to offer on the episode at Beaver Dams and the heroine who had saved her grandfather's life, but this did not prove to be so. Her account of Laura Secord's walk repeated what had already been told with the addition of a few imaginative details of her own. Here is a sample. "Clad only in a short flannel skirt and cotton jacket, without shoes or stockings, her milking stool in one hand, her pail in the other, she [Mrs. Secord] drove one of the cows close to the American lines." As documentation, the author published the now familiar FitzGibbon certificate of 1837. Because of the relationship between the author and Fitz-Gibbon, it may be assumed that a large part of the reading public accepted Miss FitzGibbon's version as factual, though it seems incredible that anyone could believe that Mrs. Secord was either so poor or so foolish as to start through the woods in her bare feet.

Mrs. E. J. Thompson was convener of the Ontario Historical Society's monument committee that was instrumental in having the Laura Secord memorial erected at Lundy's Lane. Later, Mrs. Thompson prepared a paper, "Laura Ingersoll Secord," for the Niagara Historical Society, which the society published in 1913. In her paper, Mrs. Thompson added to the Laura Secord lore with some anecdotes told by former acquaintances or relatives of the heroine; and she contributed information on Laura's children and their descendants. She gave a fanciful description of Mrs. Secord's clothing on the day she walked to Beaver Dams. According to her, the heroine wore "balbriggan stockings, with red silk clocks on the side, and low shoes with buckles." An item of interest was that "Capt. James Cummings of Chippawa always honored Laura Secord's birthday — September 13th — by hoisting the flag." Cummings, it will be remembered, was formerly the Warden of Welland county and the man from whom Laura had bought her Chippawa house.

Janet Carnochan was the outstanding local historian of the Niagara area. She contributed frequently to historical meetings and journals, always endeavouring to get at the historic truth about her subject, including Laura Secord and her walk. When the Laura Secord monument was unveiled on Queenston Heights, Miss Carnochan, who was then president of the Niagara Historical Society, read some verses she had written on the heroine. She was active in getting the Memorial Hall at Niagara-on-the-Lake erected in 1906 to commemorate the early settlers of Niagara, and to serve as a historical museum. One display case in the museum is devoted to Laura Secord, and the museum also contains a genealogical record of the Secord family and other items of related interest.

The women of Queenston felt that a serious gap still existed in the monuments to Laura Secord. While the two at Lundy's Lane and Queenston Heights spoke eloquently of their heroine, the village of Queenston had done nothing special, though this had been her home for over thirty years and this was where her famous walk had originated. The Women's Institute of Queenston and St. David's took the matter in hand, and after years of fund-raising, built a Memorial Hall as part of the Laura Secord School in Queenston. The school, erected in 1914, was originally two-roomed but now has an addition at the rear. It is an attractive red brick building with a neo-classic porch. On the stone base below the pillars at one side of the porch is a plaque that reads:

LAURA SECORD MEMORIAL / IN LOVING AND HONORED MEMORY OF / LAURA INGERSOLL SECORD / A RESIDENT OF QUEENSTON AND / A HEROINE OF UPPER CANADA / WHO SAVED HER COUNTRY / FROM THE ENEMY IN 1813.

Inside the hall, paintings of scenes from Laura Secord's life adorn the walls.

By 1914, when the First World War broke out, Laura Secord had become famous indeed. It was a sure indication of the place she held in the hearts of the Canadian people when Senator Frank O'Connor of Toronto chose her name for his new brand of chocolates. The Laura Secord Candy Shops, founded in 1913, became an extensive chain represented in a number of cities by white cottage-style shops. The candies were merchandised in white boxes adorned with a portrait of a grand-motherly Mrs. Secord and bearing the name "Laura Secord" in a stylized form of the heroine's own signature. In recent years the design of the boxes has been changed. A pretty young girl in an oval frame has replaced Mrs. Secord's likeness on the boxes which now come in a variety of shapes and colours.

It was said earlier that when you mentioned Laura Secord to people they think immediately of the woman with the cow; but this is true only in the historical context. Mention Laura Secord to the man in the street and the chances are his thoughts will turn to chocolates.

11 / THE
DEBUNKERS
TRY TO TOPPLE
LAURA

The 1920s, that lively decade following the First World War, found Laura Secord at the peak of her fame as a great Canadian heroine — the greatest, some said. Extolled in poetry, an heroic figure in the history books, commemorated in marble and bronze, her portrait hung in Ontario's hall of fame — the heroine who had remained unknown and unsung for half a century, now seemed immortal. But as the gay twenties turned to the dreary thirties, chilly winds blew across Laura's lofty heights, and the ensuing storm threatened to topple the heroine from her pedestal.

The storm took the form of a newspaper controversy stirred up by two books. Both books were written by William Stewart Wallace, then librarian of the University of Toronto and a highly respected author and historian. The first book raised the alarm because of its negative attitude to Laura Secord; the second was devastatingly positive.

In 1930 the Ontario Minister of Education authorized for use in schools *A History of the Canadian People*, by W. Stewart Wallace. In the ten pages devoted to the War of 1812, not a word was said about Laura Secord. Her name did not appear in the brief account of the Battle of Beaver Dams.

When the omission was discovered by loyal admirers of the great Canadian heroine, they were up in arms. The *Toronto Daily Star* stimulated the controversy by a front page story on December 1, 1931 reporting an interview with Mr. Wallace in which he said, "To my mind the walk [*i.e.* Laura's] was really without historical significance." He believed that FitzGibbon "had been warned by the Indians of the expected American attack before Laura Secord arrived."

Letters of protest began arriving at all four Toronto newspapers, and some editors wrote pieces in defence of Laura's claim to heroism. The *Evening Telegram* conceded that "Laura Secord's feat may not have been important to Canada's defenders of long ago, but," it went on, "it has not been without its importance to Canada that her pioneers were of such valorous stock. The story of Laura Secord is less a tale of personal achievement than a record of the spirit which imbued those who braved the toil and dangers of the early days of this country." The *Globe* declared that "the story of Laura Secord is too deeply seated in the Canadian mind to be removed now. It is part of the national heritage, a rightful possession of a people not yet surrendered to the 'debunkers.' "

One of the most persistent and convincing of the correspondents to the *Mail and Empire* was Henry Cartwright Secord, a descendant of Stephen Secord's. He quoted FitzGibbon's 1837 certificate and other sources to refute Wallace's opinion. But Wallace did not retract. As President Harry S. Truman might have said, he showed he could stand the heat of the kitchen and he spoke out even more strongly than before. In a letter to the *Mail and Empire* on December 30, 1931, he said bluntly,

As for the idea that Laura Secord "saved the

situation" at the battle of Beaver Dams, it is too absurd for serious discussion. It is dismissed by the most recent writers (both Canadian and American) on the War of 1812, and I venture to believe that any competent historical scholar who examines the evidence will be forced to pronounce it a myth.

To clinch his arguments and put his case on the record, Mr. Wallace produced a small book entitled *The Story of Laura Secord: A Study in Historical Evidence,* which was published early in 1932.* It came like an icy blast, chilling the hero-worshippers of Laura Secord.

Logically and with admirable detachment, Wallace refuted the claim that Mrs. Secord had rendered an important service to her country. He pointed out that none of the early historians of the War of 1812 had mentioned her and that Fitz-Gibbon himself had said nothing of her in his official report of June 24, 1813 on the battle of that day. He had said only that he had received information about the American advance "at seven o'clock this morning." Ducharme's report confirmed that Indians had brought this information. Wallace argued further that even in the certificate which FitzGibbon had written for Mrs. Secord in 1837, he did not state explicitly that he had received his first warning of the impending attack from her. Finally, Wallace declared that FitzGibbon's testimony was itself open to question, since he had admitted that he wrote "this Certificate in a Moment of much hurry & from Memory."

Mr. Wallace did not deny that Laura Secord had walked to FitzGibbon's headquarters, but he maintained that her walk had been futile. He based his

---

*Toronto, Macmillan.

argument on the time factor. If Mrs. Secord had left her home on the morning of June 23, as was commonly believed, she must have known about the American plan even before the leader of the expedition, Colonel Boerstler, since he had received his marching orders only on the afternoon of the twenty-third. Granted that this was possible and that Laura had gone to Beaver Dams that day, what use had FitzGibbon made of the information? Wallace's answer was "none." Had FitzGibbon not said his warning came from the Indians? On the other hand, if Mrs. Secord had gone to Beaver Dams on the twenty-fourth, Wallace argued, it was obvious she had arrived too late to be of use.

Wallace also revealed the flaw in Laura Secord's own account of her walk, already mentioned in Chapter 5, namely that she had encountered American sentries. He quoted Colonel Boerstler's testimony at his court hearing in 1815, to the effect that the Americans had withdrawn to Fort George from Queenston two days before Boerstler's expedition, and "the picquets of the American Army covered ground to the extent of two miles in front of Fort George and no more." As for the cow, Wallace singled out William F. Coffin as the inventor of that episode.

Mr. Wallace concluded that Mrs. Secord had undoubtedly taken a message to FitzGibbon, which she believed to be important, and in so doing she had shown courage and patriotism, but, he said, her message had played no part in the victory at Beaver Dams.

The Laura Secord admirers were dismayed by the evidence Mr. Wallace had assembled. One eminent book critic, William Arthur Deacon of the *Mail and Empire*, succumbed entirely to Wallace's arguments. He headed his review of the historian's booklet, "Goodbye Laura Secord." Deacon declared that "Mr. Wallace proves satisfactorily that whatever she did had no effect on the battle or on the fortunes of Canada," and he concluded, "So, as a woman of Destiny, Mrs. Secord leaves history."

It was true that, as Wallace had suggested in his letter to the *Mail and Empire*, some historians, for years past, had viewed with skepticism the claims made for Laura by her over-enthusiastic admirers. Colonel William Wood and Louis L. Babcock were two such historians. Babcock, an American, had admitted in his book *The War of 1812 on the Niagara Frontier*, published in 1927,[*] that Mrs. Secord might have tried to give warning to the British, but, he said, "it seems fairly clear that her good intentions were fruitless."

Colonel William Wood had reached a similar conclusion. He was the editor of a three-volume set of historical documents relating to the War of 1812 and published by the Champlain Society in the 1920s. In his "Introduction" to the first volume, Colonel Wood considered the events surrounding the Battle of Beaver Dams and Laura Secord's walk and he stated his opinion that "FitzGibbon had the same news from the Indians before she arrived; and the result would have been the same without her." When Wallace's booklet was published, Colonel Wood reviewed it in the *Canadian Historical Review* of March, 1932, and, with obvious relish, said, "If, after this, the public still wants a Laura Secord who 'saved the country' in 1813, it must go exclusively to those writers of alluring fiction whose works will not sell at all unless they drag some woman in." So much for historical objectivity!

Not everyone capitulated to Wallace. The *Globe* stated editorially, "There can be no doubt she

[*]Buffalo, N.Y., Buffalo Historical Society.

[Laura Secord] performed the journey for the definite purpose of warning the British and that she remains a great Canadian heroine."

The Laura Secord devotees clung fast to their faith in Laura's own words and the testimony of James FitzGibbon. Before long their faith was rewarded through the efforts of Henry Cartwright Secord. He discovered an early certificate written for Laura Secord by James FitzGibbon in 1820, only seven years after the Battle of Beaver Dams. Mr. Secord sent a copy of the certificate with a covering letter to Fred Williams, the columnist of the *Mail and Empire* who had already given generously of his space to the Secord controversy. Williams published certificate and letter in his column on June 23, 1934. The certificate, dated York, 26 February, 1820, said:

I certify that Mrs. Secord wife of James Secord of Queenston, Esquire, did in the Month of June 1813 come to the Beaver dam and communicate to me information of an intended attack to be made by the Enemy upon the Detachment then under my command, there, which occasionally occupied a large Stone House at that place. This information was Substantially correct, and a detachment did march for the Beaver Dam (on the Morning of the Second day after the information was given) under the Command of Lt. Colonel Boerstler, which Detachment was captured. Mrs. Secord arrived at my Station about Sunset of an excessibly [*sic*] warm day, after having walked twelve miles, which I at the time thought was an exertion which a person of her Slender frame and delicate appearance was unequal to make.

This certificate added little to FitzGibon's testimony of 1837, but since it was written years earlier and said substantially the same thing, it confirmed the truth of his evidence. The 1820 certificate had one additional statement of significance. The attack had come "on the morning of the second day after the information was given," said FitzGibbon. He did not give a specific date for Laura's walk, but if the day she came was considered the first day, and the day of the battle the second, then she must have taken her message on June 23, as most people had assumed.

It was still possible to argue that Laura's walk had been in vain. At the same time the publication of the 1820 certificate revealed surprising inadequacy in Mr. Wallace's research, for Mr. Secord had found this certificate in the most likely of places — the Public Archives of Canada. Furthermore it had been published ten years previously by the Niagara Historical Society in a paper entitled "Laura Secord's Walk to Warn FitzGibbon."* Captain Fitz-Gibbon had written the certificate for Mrs. Secord to support her husband's petition of February 25, 1820, for occupation of part of the military reserve at Queenston, mentioned in an earlier chapter. (It is not certain why the 1837 certificate was written, but the first known use of it was to support Mrs. Secord's petition for the concession of the Queenston ferry in 1840.)

Soon another supporter spoke out in Laura's defence. This was William Perkins Bull, in his book *From Brock to Currie* (1935), one of a series on the history of Peel county. In a lengthy appendix, the author presented "Documents Regarding Laura Secord's Trip to Beaver Dams," a compilation of evidence which was quite as impressive as Wallace's but leading to the opposite conclusion.

*By Janet Carnachan.

126

Mr. Wallace, himself, without making any admission of error, seemed to retreat from his stand in his *Encyclopaedia of Canada* which he edited, 1935-37. The article on Laura Secord described her as "heroine" and stated non-controversially that, "In the summer of 1813, while American troops were billeted in her house at Queenston, she came into possession of knowledge of American plans for a surprise attack on Beaver Dams; and she made her way through the American lines, and warned Lieut. James FitzGibbon, in command at Beaver Dams, of the projected attack."

The historical debunkers subsided, but now the art debunkers came to the fore. That portrait in Ontario's hall of fame — was there not something unusual about the face? Had Laura Secord really looked so masculine? Whispers had been heard in Queen's Park for years, and at last the talk led to action. In February, 1936, an art expert turned an x-ray eye on the portrait with intriguing results. As the Toronto *Evening Telegram* reported, "Now, through the uncanny insight of x-ray, it has been disclosed that what was seen was not only a portrait of Laura Secord but also a picture of the late Sir George Ross, his noble brow crowned with a frilly white cap." Newspaper photographs showed the "bearded Laura" (or the "bonneted Sir George") and the story came out that Mildred Peel had painted the portrait of Laura Secord over an old portrait of the Ontario Premier. He had disliked his portrait and he, or his government, had refused to pay for it.

In utilizing the discarded canvas Miss Peel followed a time-honoured practice of painters. It is an economical method, and if handled properly the original painting detracts in no way from the painting that is superimposed on the canvas. Unfortunately Miss Peel's painting failed this test.

Laura's portrait was not a fake (though it was not a good likeness) but it caused so much amusement that Laura Secord herself became the butt of quips and jokes. Premier Mitchell Hepburn decided to leave the portrait hanging, but later it was taken down and relegated to storage.

Where did the two controversies leave Laura Secord, the heroine? Nothing is more fatal to eminence than ridicule, and Laura was the victim of it from two directions — historically and artistically. The cow, the milkpail, the midnight trek through the woods in bare feet, had stretched the credulity of serious historians and had rendered suspect the entire story of Laura's heroic walk. As seen by one historian, J. K. Johnson, Mrs. Secord was a comic figure because she had "braved unspeakable dangers to tell him [FitzGibbon] something he already knew."* The exposé of the portrait heightened the impression of Laura as a comic figure.

The subject was soon forgotten when Canadians were plunged into the Second World War in 1939. For two decades they had few thoughts for the heroine of a war long past. But the story of Laura Secord was not yet ended. A key piece of evidence was still to be revealed.

In 1959, a third certificate written by James Fitz-Gibbon for Laura Secord, was discovered in the Public Archives at Ottawa. This certificate was written on May 11, 1827. It was FitzGibbon's second testimonial but it was the most important of the three because it contained the answers to two mysteries: the date of Laura's walk, and FitzGibbon's response to her message. Here is what he said:

I do hereby Certify that on the 22d day of June

*"Colonel James FitzGibbon and the Suppression of Irish Riots in Upper Canada," *Ontario History,* LVIII (1966), p. 139.

1813, Mrs. Secord, Wife of James Secord, Esq'r, then of St. David's, came to me at the Beaver Dam after Sun Set, having come from her House at St. Davids by a circuitous route a distance of twelve miles, and informed me that her Husband had learnt from an American officer the preceding night that a Detachment from the American Army then in Fort George would be sent out on the following morning (the 23rd) for the purpose of Surprising and Capturing a Detachment of the 49th Regt. then at the Beaver Dam under my command. In consequence of this information I placed the Indians under Norton together with my own Detachment in a Situation to intercept the American Detachment, and we occupied it during the night of the 22d — but the Enemy did not come until the morning of the 24th when his Detachment was captured.

Colonel Boerstler, their commander, in a conversation with me fully confirmed the information communicated to me by Mrs. Secord, and accounted for the attempt not having been made on the 23'd as at first intended.

The weather on the 22d was very hot, and Mrs. Secord whose person was slight and delicate appeared to have been and no doubt was very much exhausted by the exertion she made in coming to me, and I have ever since held myself personally indebted to her for her conduct upon that occasion, and I consider it an imperative duty on my part humbly and earnestly to recommend her to the favorable consideration of His Majesty's Provincial Government.

I beg leave to add that Mrs. Secord and her Family were entire Strangers to me before the 22d of June 1813, her exertions therefore could have been made from public motives only.

The date was now fixed: Laura had gone to Fitz-Gibbon on June 22, 1813. He had then taken suitable steps to meet the American attack. Fitz-Gibbon's memory was at fault, however, in referring to Lieutenant Norton of the Mohawks, as being in charge at Beaver Dams. Documents show that the officers were Captains William J. Kerr and Dominique Ducharme. FitzGibbon was also under the mistaken impression, mentioned previously, that the Secords lived at St. David's. But the main points regarding Laura Secord's walk were clarified in the 1827 certificate.

There could no longer be any doubt that Laura Secord had taken the warning of the planned American attack to FitzGibbon, but she had gone a day earlier than anyone had thought. It was now clear that hers was the first warning FitzGibbon had received, and that he had taken appropriate action "in consequence of this information." It was true enough that the Indian scouts had brought word of the advance on the morning of the twenty-fourth, but they had been sent out expressly to reconnoitre *because an attack was expected.* On the previous day, as has been mentioned, Ducharme had gone to Queenston on a scouting expedition for the same purpose. The Indians were ready for battle and thus were able to ambush the Americans. The outcome might have been quite different if Laura had not brought the advance warning. The British might have been ambushed rather than the Americans.

The discovery of the 1827 certificate received little publicity and created no stir. More than twenty-five years had passed since the Laura Secord controversy, and the postwar generation was concerned about more pressing problems. The Ontario Historical Society published the certificate in *Ontario History* in 1959 along with an explanatory article by John S. Moir,* a history professor, who was then at Carleton University, Ottawa. It seems odd indeed that Professor Moir did not recognize this document as a vindication of the claim that Laura Secord had made the victory possible at Beaver Dams. According to him, there was still a contradiction about when FitzGibbon had received his warning, and Professor Moir reached the strange conclusion that "this new document seems to confound rather than clarify confusion."

More recently, the military historian, J. Mackay Hitsman, in his book *The Incredible War of 1812* which appeared in 1965, accepted as factual that Laura Secord took the warning to FitzGibbon on June 22, 1813 but he suggested that since Mrs. Secord could not provide details of the American plans, FitzGibbon could only "await developments."

We have FitzGibbon's own word for it in the 1827 certificate, that he did not wait passively. He placed the Indians and his own detachment "in a Situation to intercept the American Detachment." When the attack did not come that night, Ducharme went to Queenston with some Indians the next morning to see if he could discover any sign of action. It seems certain, too, that FitzGibbon notified Colonel Bisshopp of the warning Laura Secord had brought and that Bisshopp followed this up by discussing with Major De Haren the action that should be taken in the event of an attack. Why else did Colonel Bisshopp commend De Haren, in his report on the Battle of Beaver Dams, for "his speedy movement to the point of attack and execution of the arrangements I had previously made with him"?**

---

*"An Early Record of Laura Secord's Walk," *Ontario History,* LI (1959), pp. 105-8.

**See p. 66.

The evidence is clear that Laura Secord *was* the first to bring warning to FitzGibbon of the impending attack, and that he *did* take the necessary precautions. The victory at Beaver Dams was the result.

Some people have wondered why FitzGibbon wrote three certificates for Laura. Each one was written at Mrs. Secord's request to support a petition for some appointment or other government favour. It seems likely that, with her inexperience in such matters, Laura Secord sent the original 1820 and 1827 certificates to the government without keeping copies for herself. Thus they became buried in government files. On the back of the 1827 certificate, an official (John Beverley Robinson) wrote the confidential note that has already been quoted.* He wrote the note for the information of the Lieutenant-Governor, Sir John Colborne, when Mrs. Secord wanted to become keeper of Brock's monument, advising him that "in 1827, Mr. Secord was an applicant for some situation which His Exc'y Sir P. Maitland did not find it convenient to give him." No doubt FitzGibbon wrote the certificate to support James Secord's 1827 application for the desired situation.

By 1837, Laura Secord had apparently learned that it's a wise woman who keeps copies of documents she sends to government officials. Consequently she was able to provide a copy of Fitz-Gibbon's 1837 certificate whenever she needed evidence of her walk to Beaver Dams, as, for instance, to accompany her letter to the *Anglo-American Magazine*. And thus it happened that the latest certificate, though the least important of the three, became the best known. The one that finally solved the puzzle concerning her walk, was made

*See pp. 75, 76.

public at a time and in such a manner that it created little interest. Nevertheless the discovery of the 1827 certificate reaffirmed Laura Secord's place in history.

The debunkers had shaken Laura on her pedestal but they had not toppled her.

EPILOGUE:
LAURA SECORD
AS HEROINE

Now that the mystery surrounding Laura Secord's walk has been dispelled, the question may be asked: what is her place in history? Is she entitled to be called "heroine"?

To be worthy of the name, a heroine must show exceptional courage and her heroic deed must have genuine significance. How does Laura Secord measure up?

There is no doubt about Laura's courage. Voluntarily and well aware of the dangers, she left her home and family to go on a mission that might mean capture or death. It matters little whether there actually were American sentries or not. Laura *thought* there were and she expected to encounter them, but she took the risk all the same. She was even more afraid of meeting unfriendly Indians and when she walked into the Indian encampment she feared the worst had happened. But she did not panic. She explained her mission and obtained the help of the Indian chief. Her long walk through the fields and woods invited fears of a different kind, for the danger from rattle snakes and wild animals was far from imaginary. Nor was it any small feat to walk twenty miles over rough and soggy gound on a hot day in June. Boerstler's troops complained of fatigue and hunger two days later when marching little more than half the distance over a well-travelled road. Despite all her fears and the physical endurance her task demanded, Laura Secord did not waver. She delivered her message to FitzGibbon.

How important was this message? It led to the victory at Beaver Dams, as we have seen, so the real question is: how significant was the victory? By turning the tables on the Americans, the victory took the initiative away from them in the Niagara theatre of war in 1813 and gave the British the upper hand. It prevented further advances by the Americans that year and rescued the people of the Niagara Peninsula from the hated American occupation.

To say that Laura Secord saved Canada from falling into American hands, as some of her very zealous admirers have claimed, is to exaggerate the importance of the Niagara frontier. It was an important sector, certainly, but historians are generally agreed that the naval struggle on the Great Lakes and Lake Champlain was the crucial factor in the outcome of the war. Whoever controlled the St. Lawrence River and the Great Lakes could control the interior, for this waterway was the vital artery of communications and supply.

Wars are won by a combination of factors — economic and psychological as well as military — and it takes more than one battle to decide the issue. Laura Secord played an essential part in winning one important battle in the War of 1812. Thus, in the chain of events that brought the war to an end (without a clear-cut victory on either side), Laura Secord was undoubtedly a key figure. This entitles her to a place of honour in Canadian history. In performing her historic deed, Laura displayed outstanding courage and endurance and consequently merits the title of heroine.

In her old age Laura Secord said, "I have ever found the brave and noble FitzGibbon a friend to me." Let him have the last word. His granddaughter, Mary Agnes FitzGibbon, quoted him as saying of Laura Secord, "Thus did a young, delicate woman brave the terrors of the forest in a time of such desultory warfare that the dangers were increased tenfold, to do her duty to her country, and by timely warning save much bloodshed and disaster."*

*_A Veteran of 1812,_ p. 84.

INDEX

141